Love, Life, and Lust in Heinrich Kaufringer's Verse Narratives

MEDIEVAL AND RENAISSANCE
TEXTS AND STUDIES

VOLUME 467

_____

MRTS TEXTS FOR TEACHING

VOLUME 9

Love, Life, and Lust in
Heinrich Kaufringer's Verse Narratives

ALBRECHT CLASSEN

ARIZONA CENTER FOR MEDIEVAL

ACMRS

AND RENAISSANCE STUDIES

Tempe, Arizona
2014

THE ARIZONA CENTER FOR

MEDIEVAL &
RENAISSANCE

STUDIES

Published by ACMRS (Arizona Center for Medieval and Renaissance Studies)
Tempe, Arizona

Library of Congress Cataloging-in-Publication Data

Kaufringer, Heinrich, active 14th century, author.
  [Works. Selections. English]
  Love, life, and lust in Heinrich Kaufringer's verse narratives / Albrecht Classen
[introductory notes and translation].
      pages cm. -- (Medieval and Renaissance texts and studies ; volume 467)
(MRTS texts for teaching ; volume 9)
  Includes bibliographical references and index.
  ISBN 978-0-86698-520-8 (alk. paper)
1. Kaufringer, Heinrich, active 14th century--Translations into English.
I. Classen, Albrecht, translator. II. Title.
  PT1551.K4A24 2015
  831'.3--dc23

                                                              2014045764

Cover Art:
Misericord, Cathedral of Ulm, Germany

∞
This book is made to last. It is set in Adobe Caslon Pro,
smyth-sewn and printed on acid-free paper to library specifications.
Printed in the United States of America

TABLE OF CONTENTS

INTRODUCTION

Late Medieval German Literature, *vii*
   Literary and Social-Historical Background, *x*
      Who was Heinrich Kaufringer?, *x*

Manuscripts and Textual Reception, *xiv*
   Literary-Historical Perspectives, *xv*
   The Manuscript Tradition, *xvi*
   Brief Outline of the Recent Research History, *xx*

Conclusion, *xxiii*
   The Purpose of This Translation, *xxiv*
   A Few Comments on the Problem of Translating Late Medieval, *xxvi*
      German Verse Narratives

KAUFRINGER'S VERSE NARRATIVES

No. 1: *The Hermit and the Angel*, 1
No. 2: *The Converted Jew*, 7
No. 3: *The Peasant Who Was [Falsely] Accused*, 11
No. 4: *The Mayor and the Prince*, 19
No. 5: *Payment for Love Service Returned*, 25
No. 6: *The Cowardly Husband*, 33
No. 7: *The Monk as Love Messenger, B*, 37
No. 8: *The Search for the Happily Married Couple*, 43
No. 9: *The Canon and the Cobbler*, 49
No. 10: *The Pants Left Behind*, 53

No. 11: *Three Clever Women, B,* 55

No. 12: *The Tithe on Love,* 61

No. 13: *The Revenge of the Husband,* 65

No. 14: *The Innocent Murderess,* 73

No. 15: *The Fur-Lined Blanket,* 83

No. 16: *The Three Temptations of the Devil,* 85

No. 17: *The Pious Miller's Wife,* 95

No. 18: *The Devil and the Wandering Scholar,* 101

No. 19: *Turning Away from the World,* 105

No. 20: *The Paid Lawyer,* 109

No. 21: *The Half Blanket,* 113

No. 22: *The Good Deeds,* 115

No. 23: *Merchants in Disagreement,* 117

No. 24: *The Evil and Worldly-Wise [Unscrupulous] Counselors,* 121

No. 25: *The Seven Deadly Sins,* 123

No. 26: *The Worldly Sorrows,* 127

No. 27: *God's Four Daughters,* 131

No. 28: *Disputation with a Jew about the Eucharist,* 133

No. 29: *Fight over Love and Beauty,* 137

No. 30: *New Foolishness in Fashion,* 139

No. 31: *The Councilors in the Cities,* 143

No. 32: *The Twelve Properties of Wine,* 145

Bibliography, 149

Index, 155

INTRODUCTION[1]

Late Medieval German Literature

One of the intriguing phenomena in late-medieval literature was the rise of a new genre of short verse narratives that often had a specific entertaining purpose, such as poking fun at people, but pursued, simultaneously, specific didactic intentions. Famous authors such as Giovanni Boccaccio, Geoffrey Chaucer, Franco Sacchetti, Poggio Bracciolini, and Marguerite de Navarre created a solid corpus of such narratives in the various vernaculars, such as the *Decameron* (Boccaccio), the *Canterbury Tales* (Chaucer), or the *Heptaméron* (Marguerite). These short verse narratives are characterized by their thematic orientation, regularly treating erotic themes, moral shortcomings, marital problems, and similar problems. Despite the impression that German writers were not engaged in writing similar narratives, the opposite is actually the case. As numerous editions and critical studies have demonstrated, this genre at large—difficult to define in very specific terms[2]—was highly popular in Germany already in the thirteenth century, beginning with The Stricker, and witnessed a tremendous growth well into the fifteenth century.[3]

---

[1] Sections of this introduction I copy, apart from some adaptations and expansion, from my own article, "Was There a German 'Geoffrey Chaucer' in the Late Middle Ages? The Rediscovery of Heinrich Kaufringer's Verse Narratives as Literary Masterpieces," *Studia Neophilologica* 85.1 (2013): 57–72. It is my honor to acknowledge the considerable help which I received from the German Academic Exchange Service (DAAD) through a Summer Research Grant in June and July of 2013 which allowed me to dedicate a long uninterrupted stretch of time to this research project. I am very thankful for this extraordinary support of fundamental research and of this philological translation project.

[2] There are at least four different approaches in the effort to define the genre, which my definition, in a way, merges quite deliberately; see Joachim Heinzle, "Kleine Anleitung," 1988, 45–48; see also the other contributions in that volume. For additional contributions to the huge debate as to the definition of this genre, see the references in the following notes.

[3] See, for instance, Arend Mihm, *Überlieferung und Verbreitung*, 1967; Karl-Heinz Schirmer, *Stil- und Motivuntersuchungen*, 1969; Ingrid Strasser, *Vornovellistisches Erzählen*, 1989; Hans-Joachim Ziegeler, *Erzählen im Spätmittelalter*, 1985.

According to the scholarly consensus, the *mære* is a short verse narrative with four-stressed rhyming couplets consisting of ca. 150 to ca. 2000 verses, mostly of a secular content. The themes prove to be significantly complex, thus differentiating them from similar types such as the *exemplum*, the *jest narrative* (*Schwank*), the *miracle account*, or the *fable*. *Mæren* (pl.) generally appear in larger collections and were not published by themselves in unique manuscripts. Often the authors of *mæren* question ethical norms and values and illustrate problematic situations in the protagonists' lives.[4] In other words, many of the German *mæren* authors pursued thematically idiosyncratic topics and demonstrated a remarkable creativity without ignoring altogether the larger European context, often borrowing from their predecessors and contemporaries and developing their material further.[5]

The Stricker (ca. 1220 to ca. 1250; an author whose name begins with the article; the name meaning something like 'the rope maker' of 'knitter') is particularly famous for having invented the fictional figure of the Pfaffe Amîs (Priest Amis),[6] who successfully defends himself in a number of successive verse narratives against attacks by his envious bishop and later also causes all kinds of mischief, victimizing his foolish and gullible fellow human beings, thereby becoming a model for the later character of Till Eulenspiegel, who first appeared on the literary stage in 1510.[7] Between the thirteenth and the fifteenth centuries many German writers turned their attention to this genre, the *mære*, which proved to be most convenient for the public discussion of ethical, moral, and sometimes also religious and political issues. In most cases, however, these verse narratives, as we also observe in English, French, or Italian literature, focused on erotic issues, especially problems within marriage (adultery), but also with human frailty and ignorance. We commonly hear of smart and intelligent individuals who know how to handle a difficult situation and turn it around to their advantage. More often than not, we encounter sly wives who operate quite trickily and know how to deceive their boorish and ignorant husbands. The audience is regularly invited to laugh over the duped victims, but most *mæren* also contain didactic messages.

It would not be too far-fetched to identify as important sources both for German and contemporary European verse narratives the collection of *exempla* by the Castilian priest Petrus Alfonsi, his *Disciplina clericalis* (early twelfth

---

[4] Hans-Joachim Ziegeler, "Maere," 2000.

[5] See, for example, the contributions to *The Making of the Couple*, 1991; Klaus Grubmüller, *Die Ordnung*, 2006.

[6] For a good online bibliography, see http://de.wikipedia.org/wiki/Der_Stricker.

[7] Michael Resler, "Der Stricker," 1994. For *Eulenspiegel*, see Albrecht Classen, *The German Volksbuch*, 1995.

century),[8] and John of Capua's *Directorium vitae humanae* (ca. 1263–1278). The latter in turn had been based on the Arabic *Kalfla wa-Dimna* (eighth century C.E.), and that in turn had been a translation from the ancient Indian *Panchatantra*, or *Pañcatantra* (third century B.C.E.).[9] Moreover, we also need to consider the history of medieval clerical literature as it emerged in monasteries, often characterized by witticism, satire, and irony, which could have influenced both the Old French *fabliaux* and the Middle High German *mæren*.[10]

Curiously, if we compare many of the larger collections with Middle High German *mæren* produced after The Stricker's *Pfaffe Amîs* with those compilations that are identified by the name of an author and narrator, whose intradiegetic presence provides a considerable cohesion to the anthology, such as Chaucer's *Canterbury Tales*, the absolute dearth of relevant figures in the Germanic area seems rather striking at first. Perhaps the only remarkable but very little studied exception might be the *Buch der Beispiele der alten Weisen* by Anton von Pforr (d. 1483). Significantly, that *Buch* is an indirect German translation of the Indian *Pañcatantra* (ca. 200–300/400 C.E.) via the Latin translation by John of Capua (1263–1278), his *Directorium vitae humanae* (see above), which intriguingly closes the circle of narrative dependencies, influences, borrowings, translations, and imitations. In essence, of course, all these writers, from ancient times to the late Middle Ages, pursued didactic, moral, and ethical purposes embedded in popular forms of entertainment.[11]

This puzzling situation of the absence of a German writer/poet comparable to Boccaccio or Chaucer is not the result of a simple oversight, but apparently a characteristic feature of fifteenth-century German literature, at least pertaining to that genre. By contrast, when we consider the situation in the following centuries, completely different conditions seem to dominate, since we can point to such major authors as Johannes Pauli, Georg (Jörg) Wickram, Hans Wilhelm Kirchhof, Michael Lindener, Valentin Schuhmann, Wilhelm Frey, and others, all of them composing many prose narratives or *Schwänke* by then. Those authors embedded their collections in a narrative framework with a prologue and epilogue, or interjected personal opinions similar to those we find them in other

---

[8] For Petrus Alfonsi, see John Tolan, *Petrus Alfonsi*, 1993. Some of the online reference works prove to be quite impressive; see, for instance, http://en.wikipedia.org/wiki/Petrus_Alphonsi; for his *Disciplina Clericalis*, see: http://en.wikipedia.org/wiki/Disciplina_Clericalis#Works_in_Disciplina_Clericalis (last accessed on Sept. 5, 2014).

[9] http://en.wikipedia.org/wiki/Panchatantra (with a good bibliography up to 2011; last accessed on Sept. 5, 2014). For the literary-historical context, focusing on the German tradition, see Klaus Grubmüller, *Die Ordnung*, 2006, 94–111.

[10] Clemens and Gibaldi, *Anatomy of the Novella*, 1977.

[11] Sabine Obermaier, *Das Fabelbuch*, 2004.

European literatures, thereby authoritatively underscoring their predominant authority function.[12]

However, this does not mean that, in comparison, most fifteenth-century literature has come down to us anonymously; on the contrary, we know of such major figures as Oswald von Wolkenstein (d. 1445), Michel Beheim (d. ca. 1472), Hans Rosenplüt (d. ca. 1460), Hans Folz (d. 1513), and others The so-called Mönch von Salzburg (early fifteenth-century poet of religious and secular poems), however, remains a rather vague personality, the name probably serving as a mask for the bishop himself or someone in his entourage.[13] The late Middle Ages witnessed an enormous growth of large collections of songs in so-called *Liederbücher*, but here again anonymity ruled supreme.[14]

Even though we would probably look in vain for a poet like Boccaccio or Chaucer in the German-speaking lands, one name stands out that deserves further study, and this not only within German philology but on a larger level. Heinrich Kaufringer from Landsberg am Lech near Augsburg, specifically from the little village Kaufering nearby, whoever he might have been in biographical-historical terms, can be identified as one of those major figures who authored a larger number of *mæren*. He is credited with having created a collection of verse narratives that might serve, if not tantamount in volume and quality to the *Decameron* or the *Canterbury Tales*, that is, as the German representative of the great late medieval narrative tradition, of the genre of verse narrative known as *mære*. As Paul Sappler, the modern editor of Kaufringer's tales, specifies, this poet succeeded in adapting many of the well-known narrative motifs, presenting numerous figures in unusual social contexts, and in developing authentic and new motifs and themes. In later chapters, I will subsequently present an English translation of his works and hope thus to introduce a major late medieval writer to scholarship beyond the pale of German literature.

Literary and Social-Historical Background

Who was Heinrich Kaufringer?

We generally assume that this author was an urban dweller, as most of his tales are situated in a city, although it might be too audacious to characterize Kaufringer as a realistic narrator mirroring automatically an urban setting only. Moreover,

---

[12] Albrecht Classen, *Deutsche Schwankliteratur*, 2009.

[13] See the contributions to *Autorentypen*, ed. Walter Haug and Burghart Wachinger, 1991.

[14] Albrecht Classen, *Deutsche Liederbücher des 15. und 16. Jahrhunderts*, 2001; idem, (together with Lukas Richter), *Lied und Liederbuch*, 2010.

View on to the Herkommerplatz (Herkommer Square) in Landsberg am Lech

Kaufringer clearly reflects the interests and concerns of an audience situated in a city, although some of his tales also pertain to the courts, chivalry, and life in the village. He was highly learned and deeply religious, yet consistently embraced pragmatic, realistic concepts and tended to ridicule foolish peasants, while aristocrats, if they appear in his tales, tend to operate in a city. Since the fourth *mære* contains a reference to the University of Erfurt, which was founded in 1392, we must assume that the poet composed his works after that date, perhaps around 1400. After all, it must have taken some time for the reputation of the Erfurt University to spread even to southern Germany before Kaufringer could build his tale on the general awareness of that site.

The Munich manuscript (cgm 270) containing the bulk of his texts is explicitly dated with the year 1464, which gives us a good *terminus ante quem*. The ninth *mære* takes place in Augsburg, and two locations in its vicinity are also mentioned, Wiedergeltingen and Türkheim. While both names primarily serve a metaphorical purpose with allusions to cunning and the like, they are specifically identifiable geographic name. I will discuss these villages below in more detail.

Unfortunately, we do not know for sure who the author might have been because two individuals are mentioned in the records of Landsberg with that name, the older serving as a church administrator between 1369 and 1404, and the younger, probably his son, mentioned only once in a document from December 8, 1404. Kaufring itself is a village on the river Lech, four kilometers north of Landsberg. As far as the elder Kaufringer is concerned, we know that he served as testamentary witness for a Hans Angerer in Kaufbeuren who administered the payment of his brother's inheritance to his sister, Adelheid, who had the same name as Kaufringer's wife. We do not know whether there might have been any meaningful connection. Two of the main manuscripts were created in Augsburg, and Augsburg is twice the locale where a narrative takes place ("The Monk as Messenger of Love" and "The Canon and the Cobbler's Wife"). The major linguistic features of Kaufringer's texts locate him in the East Swabian area of Augsburg. In addition, he was obviously familiar with two towns near Augsburg, as we know from "The Canon and the Cobbler's Wife," once Widergeltingen (v. 116), which is 15 kilometers west of Landsberg, and once Türkheim (v. 116), 3 kilometers further west.

The lack of documentary evidence thus far makes it impossible to determine whether Kaufringer belonged to the urban patricians or to the guilds, but he might have held a position as a judge or councilor within his city, as some narrative motifs suggests, but do not confirm.[15] Ironically, however, he voiced rather harsh criticism of the clergy at large, and also viewed judges pretty negatively. Moreover, he held a very pessimistic view of city councilors and portrayed them at times as highly selfish and arrogant. Kaufringer was, altogether, a sarcastic critic of his time and did not hesitate to lash out at many different types of people, professions, and estates, although he was intimately tied to that middle class, as reflected by the fact that his name is mentioned in a number of documents from June 15, 1369 to December 8, 1404, today all housed today either in the Stadtarchiv (City Archive) Landsberg or in the Hauptstaatsarchiv (Primary State Archive) Munich.[16]

---

[15] Paul Sappler, "Kaufringer, Heinrich," 1982, 1076–78.
[16] Hanns Fischer, *Studien zur deutschen Märendichtung*, 1983, 150–51.

Old City Hall, Landsberg am Lech

Map of southern Germany

Manuscripts and Textual Reception

The Munich manuscript cgm 270, completed in 1464, contains Kaufringer's texts nos. 1–17, three of which, nos. 14, 16, and 17, are accompanied by the author's signature. The first narrative was copied a second time in 1467 in the Munich manuscript, Staatsbibliothek Munich, cgm 1119 on fol. 97vb–100ra, written by the Munich cup-bearer Jörg Werder. That manuscript also contains the narrative *Wilhalm von Orlens* and sermons by the famous Franciscan preacher Berthold von Regensburg (ca. 1210–1272), among others. The other major Kaufringer manuscript is the one held by the Staatsbibliothek Preußischer Kulturbesitz Berlin, Mgf 564, copied by the professional Augsburg scribe Konrad Bollstatter in 1472.[17] It primarily contains gnomic, or didactic, poems by The Teichner, but also ten pieces by Kaufringer, as documented by the author's signature (nos. 18–27). Five narratives allegedly signed by The Teichner and incorporated in the middle of the Kaufringer texts (nos. 91, 99, 111, 206, 209) seem rather untypical for The Teichner, as Heinrich Niewöhner, the editor of Teichner's works in

---

17 Jürgen Wolf, "Konrad Bollstatter," 1996, 51–86. Until today this manuscript has not yet been fully described, and there is no digitized version available yet either.

modern times, observed: hence, despite the Teichner signature, they might be attributed to Kaufringer.[18]

We might be still too far away from making a final decision regarding their authenticity, but the possibility, if not probability, that Kaufringer created them, even though the scribe falsely (?) assigned them to The Teichner, motivated Paul Sappler to include them in his edition of Kaufringer's works as nos. 28–32. Following Sappler, I have translated them here as well, since I lean toward accepting them as composed by Kaufringer after all. As far as we can tell, Kaufringer's verse narratives were not copied by later writers after the 1470s, when the last manuscripts containing his texts were created (see above), but in light of massive production of sixteenth century prose *Schwänke* (jest narratives), many of which drew in one or the other way from the late medieval tradition, there is still a good chance of discovering cases of later writers who might have been influenced by Kaufringer's narratives.[19]

Literary-Historical Perspectives

Kaufringer composed at least seventeen secular verse narratives, the so-called *mæren*, and a good number of religious tales, all well developed in an interesting and attention-grabbing manner.[20] Altogether there are thirty-two narratives preserved in the two manuscripts (Munich and Berlin), which he apparently composed for the entertainment of, and with some didactic and religious intentions for, his audience. He was, to be sure, not a poet dependent upon a patron and could thus pursue his literary goals fairly freely, formulating rather conservative viewpoints with respect to urban life and marriage, not to mention his ridicule of foolish peasants and clerics. At least there is no reference to any patron, no indication that the texts were commissioned, nor that these *mæren* met any specific set of ideological expectations. Kaufringer does not serve, as far as we can tell in light of his narratives, as a spokesperson for the Church or for the aristocracy. Although he often places his narratives in the city, he was not a particular defender of the urban class either. By the same token, he incorporates a number of individual characters from the higher aristocracy, yet without necessarily idealizing them. In conformity with the general trend of his time, the poet

---

[18] Heinrich Niewöhner, "Pseudoteichnerisches," 1953, 391–414. In a conversation with Hans-Joachim Ziegeler, Bonn, July 17, 2014, he confirmed with me that the scholarly consensus currently accepts the viewpoint that those narratives mixed in with The Teichner's works have to be attributed to Kaufringer.

[19] Classen, *Deutsche Schwankliteratur*, 2009. I myself did not come across any example of a *Schwank* possibly influenced by a Kaufringer model, but I had not focused on that possibility during my research then. Future research might discover such connections.

[20] Heinrich Kaufringer, *Werke*, ed. Paul Sappler. Vol. I, 1972, VII–VIII.

Karolinenbrücke (Caroline Bridge), Landsberg am Lech

happily embraced an anticlerical attitude, but he was certainly not a radical critic of the Church.

Quite typically for the situation around 1400, Kaufringer emerges as a satirical but also religious and moralistic writer who wants to entertain and instruct at the same time. In this regard his work bears many similarities with texts by such literary luminaries as the Italian Boccaccio and the English Geoffrey Chaucer, although we could not claim any direct connections or borrowings across the linguistic and geographic divide.[21]

The Manuscript Tradition

Karl Euling published the first edition of Kaufringer's *mæren* in 1883, based on the Munich manuscript cgm 270, followed by Hans Schmidt-Wartenberg in 1897 who made available ten further texts contained in the Berlin manuscript mgf 564. The modern critical edition was finally prepared by Paul Sappler in 1972.

The Munich manuscript cgm 270, comprising a total of 388 leaves, represents a very rich collection of late medieval verse narratives by a number

---

[21] Classen, "Was There a German 'Geoffrey Chaucer' in the Late Middle Ages?", 2013. For the tradition of anticlerical literature, see Birgit Beine, *Der Wolf in der Kutte*, 1999 (with many but too brief references to Kaufringer's texts).

of different writers and thus has attracted much interest by scholars.[22] It can now be viewed online as a digital copy at: http://daten.digitale-sammlungen. de/~db/0005/bsb00052961/images/ (last accessed on Sept. 5, 2014). It might be important to gain a good overview of the entire content in order to understand how Kaufringer's texts fit into that anthology. I have translated the German titles, if they do not simply carry the protagonist's name:

Ms. Munich cgm 270:
Fol. 1r–24r = 'Wilhalm von Orlens' (A)
Fol. 27r–30v = 'Lob der Frauen' I (Praise of Women)
Fol. 30v–37r = 'Die versuchte Treue' (The Tested Loyalty)
Fol. 37r–40v = 'Die Heimkehr der gefangenen Geliebten' (Return Home of the Captured Mistress)
Fol. 40v–43r = Peter Schmieher: 'Die Wolfsklage' (M1) (Lament of the Wolf)
Fol. 43v–45r = 'Minneerlebnis' (Love Adventure)
Fol. 45r–50v = 'Der Traum' (The Dream)
Fol. 50v–55r = Hans Raminger: 'Von der natur des Kindes' (M) (The Child's Nature)
Fol. 55r–57r = Hans Raminger: 'Von der armut' (M) (On Poverty)
Fol. 57r–59r = Peter Groninger: 'Von sant Sebastian' (Of Saint Sebastian)
Fol. 59v–60r = 'Stiefmutter und Tochter' (Mother-in-Law and Daughter-in-Law)
Fol. 60r–64v = Heinrich von Pforzen: 'Der Pfaffe in der Reuse' (The Priest Caught in the Fish Trap)
Fol. 67r–68v = 'Den Jungen die Minne, den Alten der Wein!' (Love Belongs to the Young People, and Wine to the Old People)
Fol. 68v–71r = Peter Suchenwirt: 'Liebe und Schönheit' (m4) (Love and Beauty)
Fol. 71r–73r = 'Des Labers Rat' (Laber's Advice)
Fol. 79v–85r = 'Der unentwegte Liebhaber' (The Untiring Lover)
Fol. 85v–92r = Der arme Konrad: 'Frau Metze' (Lady Metze)
Fol. 92r–96r = 'Streit für und gegen die Minne' (Debate for and against Love)
Fol. 96r–102r = 'Des Labers Lehren' (Laber's Teachings)
Fol. 102r–106v = 'Der Spalt in der Wand' (The Crack in the Wall)
Fol. 106v–107r = 'Klage einer jungen Frau' (Lament of a Young Woman)
Fol. 111r–119v = 'Von treulosen Männern' (Of Disloyal Men)
Fol. 121r = 'Lob der guten Fut' (Praise of the Good Vagina)
Fol. 121v–124v = 'Die Beichte einer Frau' (Confession of a Woman)

---

[22] For a detailed description of the ms. cgm 270, see Karin Schneider, *Die deutschen Handschriften der Bayerischen Staatsbibliothek München: Cgm*, 1970, 189–208. Now available online at: http://www.manuscripta-mediaevalia.de/hs/katalogseiten/HSK0043_a208_JPG.htm (last accessed on Sept. 5, 2014).

Fol. 124v–130v = Peter Suchenwirt: 'Die schöne Abenteuer' (m4) (The Beautiful Lady Adventure)

Fol. 130v–135r = 'Der Knappe und die Frau' (The Squire and the Lady)

Fol. 135r–137v = 'Die verspotteten Liebhaber' (Lovers Mocked At)

Fol. 137v–144r = 'Die getrennten Minnenden' (Lovers Separated)

Fol. 144v–147v = 'Verschwiegene Liebe' (Secret Love)

Fol. 147v–152v = 'Ironische Minnelehre' (Ironic Teaching on Love)

Fol. 152v–158r = 'Herz und Leib' (Heart and Body)

Fol. 158r–159v = 'Des Liebhabers Verabschiedung' (Good-Bye of the Lover)

Fol. 159v–160r = 'Der Landstreicher im Hurenhaus' (The Vagabond in the Brothel)—a later user/reader deliberately obliterated that text, obviously because it appeared to him as too lascivious and pornographic. But the text, of which only fragments remain, can still be read well.

Fol. 160r–164v = Fröschel von Leidnitz: 'Die Liebesprobe' (M1) (The Test of Love)

Fol. 165r–167v = 'Die sechs Farben' I (The Six Colors)

Fol. 167v–172r = 'Des Mädchens Klage um den toten Freund' (The Girl's Lament for the Dead Friend)

Fol. 172r–174v = 'Der treue Liebhaber' (The Loyal Lover)

Fol. 178r–186r = Michel (?) Gernpaß: Poetische 'Secretum secretorum'-Bearbeitung (b) (Poetic Rendering of the *Secretum secretorum*)

Fol. 191r–192v = 'Die Kupplerin' (The Go-Between)

Fol. 197v = Mönch von Salzburg: 'Das guldein ABC' (The Golden ABC)

Fol. 203r–204r = Collection of Gnomic poems by, among others, Freidank

Fol. 204v–205r = Hans Raminger: 'Die Unersättliche' (M) (The Insatiable Woman)

Fol. 205r–207v = Hans Raminger: 'Ain spruch von den meden' (A Poetic Teaching about Young Women)

Fol. 207v–208v = 'Klage über die falsche Minne' (Lament about False Love)

Fol. 210r–212r = 'Spottgedicht auf abenteuerliche Minne' (Mocking Poem on Adventurous Love)

Fol. 212r–213r = 'Bettgespräch' (Bed Talks)

Fol. 223v–232r = Freidank

Fol. 234r–388v = Heinrich Kaufringer (nos. 1–17)

The Munich ms. cgm 1119 comprises 107 leaves and contains the following texts or groups of texts[23]:

Fol. 1ra–96vb = Berthold von Regensburg: sermons (M), among these:

---

[23] For a detailed description of this ms., see Karin Schneider, *Die deutschen Handschriften*, 1991; now available online at: http://www.manuscripta-mediaevalia.de/hs/katalogseiten/HSK0189_a112_jpg.htm (last accessed on Sept. 5, 2014).

Fol. 16va–19ra = Berthold von Regensburg: 'Von den Zeichen der Messe' (Of the Signs in Mass)

Fol. 97ra–vb = Various verse and prose statements

Fol. 97vb–100ra = Heinrich Kaufringer: 'Der Einsiedler und der Engel' (The Hermit and the Angel)

Fol. 100ra–107ra = 'Wilhalm von Orlens' (B)

The Berlin ms. mgf 564 comprises 333 leaves and contains primarily the following texts, here disregarding shorter poems[24]:

Ms. Berlin mgf 564:
Heinrich der Teichner: Poems (O)

Fol. 102v–103r = 'Der König vom Odenwald,' revised by Peter Schmieher: 'Von der Kuh' (On the Cow)

Fol. 117v–120r = 'Die zwölf Trünke' (a) (The Twelve Drinks)

Fol. 126v–128v = 'Wer kann allen recht tun?' (Who Can Do It Right For Everyone)

Fol. 129v–130v = Heinrich Kaufringer: 'Die Ratsherren in den Städten' (The Councilmen in the Cities)

Fol. 143v–144r = Morgenrot, 'Spruch von Glück und des Menschen Sinn' (Poem on Happiness and the Meaning of Mankind)

Fol. 144v–147v = Heinrich Kaufringer: 'Neue Modetorheiten' (New Foolishness in Fashion)

Fol. 155r–158r = Der Teichner, 'Vom Pfennig' (On Money)

Fol. 164r–167v = Heinrich Kaufringer: 'Der Teufel und der fahrende Schüler' (The Devil and the Wandering Scholar)

Fol. 273r–275v = Heinrich Kaufringer: 'Abkehr von der Welt' (Turning Away from the World)

Fol. 276r–279r = Heinrich Kaufringer: 'Der bezahlte Anwalt' (The Paid Lawyer)

Fol. 279r–281r = Heinrich Kaufringer: 'Die halbe Decke' (The Half Blanket)

Fol. 281r–282v = Heinrich Kaufringer: 'Die guten Werke' (The Good Deeds)

Fol. 282v–285v = Heinrich Kaufringer (?): 'Disputation mit einem Juden über die Eucharistie' (Disputation with a Jew on the Eucharist)

Fol. 285v–289r = Heinrich Kaufringer: 'Die uneinigen Kaufleute' (Merchants in Disagreement)

Fol. 289r–290v = Heinrich Kaufringer: 'Die weltgewandten Bösewichter' (The Evil and World–Smart [Unscrupulous] Councilors)

Fol. 290v–292r = 'Streit über Liebe und Schönheit' (Fight over Love and Beauty)

---

[24] For a brief catalogue description, which is, however, for our purposes still unsatisfactory, see http://www.manuscripta-mediaevalia.de/hs/katalogseiten/HSK0603a_b062_jpg.htm (last accessed on Sept. 5, 2014). For a detailed listing of all texts in the ms. mgf 564, see http://www.handschriftencensus.de/4393 (last accessed on Sept. 5, 2014).

Fol. 292v–297r = Heinrich Kaufringer: 'Die sieben Hauptsünden' (The Seven
  Deadly Sins)
Fol. 327v–330r = Heinrich Kaufringer: 'Das zeitliche Leiden' (The Worldly Sor-
  rows)
Fol. 302v–304v = Der Teichner
Fol. 314r–316r = Der Teichner
Fol. 330v–333r = Heinrich Kaufringer: 'Die vier Töchter Gottes' (God's Four
  Daughters)

Considering that Kaufringer's works can be found in at least two truly important
and rich volumes of late medieval German literature that contain a large number
of contemporary texts with a wide range of genres and themes, we recognize even
further how significant this author was for his time.[25] Critics might argue that
the fairly small number of manuscripts with his texts does not necessarily support this claim, but he was certainly still known ca. 70 years after his death and
obviously enjoyed considerable respect as a noteworthy writer who had important messages to relate. Unfortunately, there is no author portrait in either one
of the manuscripts, while Der Teichner is impressively represented in the Berlin
manuscript mgf 564.

Brief Outline of the Recent Research History

Since the appearance of Sappler's edition, Kaufringer has been studied more intensively from various perspectives in comparison to the past, but modern, more
focused research only began with the monograph by Marga Stede (1993), who
believed she recognized in this poet a voice of the crisis as it deeply affected the
late Middle Ages. In her study she mostly followed previous approaches in which
the literary manifestations of the fifteenth century were compared with their
predecessors and thus understood as expressions of decline. Stede observed that
every narrative included messages about how to safeguard one's soul, although
she also granted that Kaufringer was regularly concerned with conveying fundamental teachings about everyday ethics, outlining in his *mæren* and other verse
narratives how the individual could survive successfully in the ordinary life conditions of his or her time, safeguarding both worldly happiness and the well-being of the soul in the afterlife.[26]

Despite the often pragmatic approach, the narrator regularly points out the
transcendental dimension that deeply determines the protagonist's actions.[27]

---

[25] For the latest summary of the manuscript situation, see the online database *Mar-
burger Repertorium* at http://www.handschriftencensus.de/werke/4096 (last accessed on
Sept. 5, 2014).
[26] Marga Stede, *Schreiben in der Krise*, 1993, 296–329.
[27] Stede, *Schreiben in der Krise*, 1993, 328–29.

Stede's key word in identifying Kaufringer's central intention is "Krisenbewälti-gung" (329; "coming to terms with the crisis"). Curiously, and with little justi-fication, Michaela Willers rejects this concept and insists, instead, on analyzing Kaufringer's verse narratives solely on the basis of the manuscript context, as-suming that the way in which the *mæren* were arranged by the scribe/s might re-veal specific author intentions free from any references to a global crisis. Primar-ily, however, Willers discusses Kaufringer's work as an attempt by people to cope with the complexity of their ordinary life, far removed from seeking perfection and social and legal justice. People's shortcomings are noticeable everywhere, and human error and failure dominate more than wisdom and intelligence. Ra-tionality and logic emerge as highly desirable features, but hardly anyone com-mands enough intellectual capacity or ethical and moral values to lead his or her life in a truly harmonious manner.[28]

Willers also points out that Kaufringer embraced a unique approach to law, insofar as he presents numerous cases in which worldly law, if closely but nar-rowly obeyed without considering God's true intentions, would lead to chaos and injustice in global terms.[29] But her monograph does not reach truly new perspec-tives and offers only interpretations of the individual tales that do not go much beyond traditional approaches. Considering the wide range of intriguing topics covered by this poet, including domestic violence, murder, marriage, individual happiness, and the like, it does not come as a surprise that Kaufringer continues to be somewhat neglected by research.[30]

Klaus Grubmüller suggests that Kaufringer aimed only at illustrating the power of the literary exemplum, in which the traditional application of cunning and circumspection begin to fail because they clash with the difficult conditions in reality. In this sense, Kaufringer would be, as Grubmüller believes, the one poet who deconstructs the genre of the didactic verse narrative altogether, un-dermining all hope in the application of literary discourse for the improvement of the audience. Not surprisingly, as he then concludes, Kaufringer did not ex-perience a significant reception, considering that his *mæren* have survived only in the Munich and the Berlin manuscripts.[31] But quantity of extant texts is a rather speculative criterion in the evaluation of a literary work, especially from the Middle Ages, and to suggest that the proper way of reading his *mæren* from a purely deconstructive point of view does not aid us much, especially if we con-sider Kaufringer's clearly didactic intentions.

One extreme example would be the earlier verse novella, *Mauritius von Craûn*, composed ca. 1215–1250, which was recorded only once in the *Ambraser Heldenbuch*, completed ca. 1516. Although this narrative has survived in only

[28] Michaela Willers, *Heinrich Kaufringer als Märenautor*, 2002, 288–90.
[29] Willers, *Heinrich Kaufringer*, 2002, 307–08.
[30] Classen, "Mord, Totschlag, Vergewaltigung," 2000, 3–36.
[31] Grubmüller, *Die Ordnung*, 2006, 191.

one sixteenth-century manuscript, scholarship at large has identified it today as a true masterpiece of an extraordinary kind from the late Middle Ages.[32] The quality of a literary work must rest on its intrinsic values and its power to convey meaningful messages both for its own time and subsequent generations. Like Boccaccio or Chaucer, Kaufringer's narratives succeed in appealing to us even today, being thought-provoking and insightful in many different ways. Hence they deserve to be studied much more in detail, and I hope that this English translation will contribute to bringing about a shift in research focus on late medieval German literature.

As Paul Sappler indicates, several major themes poignantly characterize Kaufringer's work and profile its idiosyncrasies. On the one hand he includes instances of several cases in which a happy marriage is preserved because the wife employs her wit and intelligence to extricate herself from highly problematic conditions, usually set up by her fortunate but not truly wise husband. Similarly, adulterous wives triumph at times over ignorant and boorish husbands, though it would go too far to state, as Klaus Grubmüller has suggested, that their violent behavior signifies the absolute dominance of completely immoral and irresponsible judgment.[33]

Peasants are not simply ridiculed here; on the contrary, again intelligence and clever behavior allow an individual, irrespective of his or her social status, to defeat even high-ranking members of the Church—all characteristic topics addressed in the entire genre of European entertaining short verse narrative since the thirteenth century.[34] Kaufringer targets many different shortcomings and failures in his society, but he never radically rejects that society, its institutions, or the fundamental structure of the late medieval world. Individuals make mistakes, as he observes, and he notices egregious tendencies here and there, but his literary comments never undermine an entire social class nor his environment. In this regard we recognize, once again, numerous parallels with contemporary European literature, whether we think of Boccaccios's *Decameron*, Chaucer's *Canterbury Tales*, or the anonymous French collection, *Cent Nouvelles Nouvelles*.[35]

I myself have discussed Kaufringer's verse narratives on several occasions, highlighting the degree to which the theme of violence, coupled with love and sexuality, enters the individual stories,[36] how much Kaufringer engages in the universal discourse on love and marriage (similar to his contemporary Chaucer),[37] and how much we can compare his work with Chaucer's *Canterbury*

---

[32] *Mauritius von Craûn*, 2000; Hubertus Fischer, *Ritter, Schiff und Dame*, 2006.

[33] Grubmüller, *Die Ordnung*, 2006, 221–22.

[34] Sappler, "Kaufringer," 1982, cols. 1082–85.

[35] Classen, "Vom Mære zum Prosa-Schwank des 16. und 17. Jahrhunderts," 2014.

[36] Classen, "Mord, Totschlag," 2000.

[37] Classen, "Love, Marriage, and Sexual Transgressions," 2004.

Tales.[38] Much remains to be done, since even German scholars have not yet fully recognized the true importance of this writer.[39] But I am convinced that this English translation will serve as a springboard for new interest by researchers and students even outside of the Germanophile scope, and hopefully also by the general reader. Kaufringer certainly deserves it, as future detailed critical analyses of individual examples will demonstrate.

Conclusion

We would have to examine each one of Kaufringer's verse narratives (both his *mæren* and his religious-didactic narratives) to do full justice to his literary accomplishments, unearthing the multiple and sometimes seemingly contradictory strategies contained in them, forcing his readers/listeners to debate the issues at stake from many different perspectives. They are rarely "einsinnig" (one-dimensional), as Willers (91) and other scholars have often argued, and it would be wrong to consider them unworthy of our critical attention, as is sometimes indicated by the general neglect that Kaufringer suffers from, although he was certainly a major writer at his time. Future literary historians will have to do justice, and I hope the present work will be an important stepping stone in that direction.[40] We should also make some concrete comparisons with Chaucer to bolster the claim that Kaufringer could be placed on the same level as his English contemporary, at least as a story teller who provokes the audience to take sides in highly complex issues involving love, marriage, and sexuality.[41] But we recognize in Kaufringer an individual who embraced tough, challenging ethical, moral, and religious issues and obviously wanted to invite his audience to reflect with him on fundamental concerns regarding human interactions and social conflicts. His responses to specific conflicts might not necessarily satisfy us or make us feel comfortable, but that would not be the task of the literary discourse in the first place.

The intention of this introduction is not to enter into any kind of comparative analysis; instead I want to state only briefly that Kaufringer succeeded in creating astoundingly complex, conflictual, and often rather daring tales in which

---

[38] Classen, "Was There a German 'Geoffrey Chaucer' in the Late Middle Ages?," 2013.

[39] Peter Nusser, *Deutsche Literatur*, vol. 1, 2012, 317–18, mentions him only in passing.

[40] Curiously, Hans-Joachim Ziegeler, *Erzählen im Spätmittelalter*, 1985, mentions him only once, 457. The same applies to Ingrid Strasser, *Vornovellistisches Erzählen*, 1989, 21, 145, 147. See also Karl-Heinz Schirmer, *Stil- und Motivuntersuchungen*, 1969, who seems to ignore Kaufringer completely.

[41] See the contributions to *Discourses on Love, Marriage, and Transgression in Medieval and Early Modern Literature*, ed. Albrecht Classen, 2004, and to *Words of Love and Love of Words in the Middle Ages and the Renaissance*, ed. Albrecht Classen, 2008.

we observe stunning contradictions between secular and spiritual perspectives, between external perception and transcendental understanding, and between human law and divine justice. Life is contingent, as we as his readers realize too often. Issues of communication emerge here as much as social and ethical concerns, and they often find surprising expression. Many times the topics of love and marriage are discussed from sometimes radically polar positions. Male identity issues often rise to the surface, especially within the framework of early-modern urban life. As entertaining as Kaufringer's narratives always prove to be, they consistently address fundamentally didactic, ethical, moral, and often also religious issues. Kaufringer emerges as a sharp and occasionally rasping observer of his world, as a conservative critic, and as an elegant literary entertainer in his own rights.

As any careful analysis can demonstrate, the author regularly challenges his audience by presenting highly complex legal conditions that do not find easy answers, thus triggering profound debates about how to evaluate individual behavior, decisions, attitudes, and values. That, in fact, represents the highest mark of literary quality; so in a way we might really be justified to identify Kaufringer, not even facetiously, as the equivalent of a German Boccaccio or Chaucer.[42] Of course, both produced many more and much more diverse types of texts; they were truly masters of their time, but within the tradition of German and European verse narratives, Kaufringer emerges as an impressive and remarkable representative who had an extraordinary grasp of how to develop intriguing, provocative, and challenging *mæren*. Nothing would be further from the truth than to claim that this author reflects on the meaninglessness of this world, although some German scholars have suggested just that in order to add a dramatic dimension to fifteenth century German literature at large in contrast to the European context.[43]

The Purpose of This Translation

While German scholars have certainly taken note of Kaufringer's *mæren*, though without acknowledging them as particularly outstanding,[44] which I would strongly contest, he has remained virtually unknown in the Anglophone or Francophone worlds, to mention just two language areas. Many of his verse narratives are short but powerful literary masterpieces that deserve considerable attention for their profound and provocative themes and messages, placing him in

---

[42] For the English translation of just a few of Kaufringer's tales, see *Erotic Tales of Medieval Germany*, 2009.

[43] Grubmüller, *Die Ordnung*, 2006, 246, even speaks of the "Orgien der Sinnlosigkeit" (Orgies of meaninglessness), which is, however, rather absurd and theory-driven.

[44] A major exception proves to be the study by Udo Friedrich, "Metaphorik des Spiels," 1996, 1–30.

City Square, Landsberg am Lech

a venerable tradition from Boccaccio to Marguerite de Navarre, but now in the German tongue. This English translation of all texts known for certain to be his and even those where the attribution might be questionable, will, I hope, close a major gap and provide the necessary springboard for many future scholars and general readers to pay closer attention to this major writer. Even if those *mæren* that were signed by The Teichner cannot be attributed to Kaufringer, then we have an additional opportunity to meet another major contemporary writer virtually unknown in the Anglophone world.

Obviously, a translation can never fully substitute for the original Middle High German text, but it can open heretofore closed doors and make it possible to incorporate Kaufringer's texts into larger comparative and interdisciplinary studies. Although his *mæren* have already been studied a number of times and been translated into modern German to some extent (see above), here I render for the first time all of his texts, including those of questionable authenticity, into English.

Several of his narratives have been translated before by Cynthia Lynn Simmons as part of her Master Thesis at the University of Texas, Austin, in 1985. These are: No. 6: "The Cowardly Husband"; No. 8: "The Search for the Happily Married Couple"; No. 9: "The Canon and the Cobbler's Wife"; and No. 14: "The Innocent Murderess." I created my translation independently of her work, but have subsequently compared my efforts with her renderings, as reflected in occasional footnotes. Overall, she created a fairly good translation, but I disagree with her decisions in a number of instances, apart from subjective, stylistic reasons, either because she translated the Middle High German too literally or too freely. Nevertheless, her English version stays close enough to the original and thus impressively met the expectations at the time when she completed her Master thesis. Simmons also studied Kaufringer's biographical background, the transmission and editions of the texts, the genre of the *mæren*, the aspect of performance, the role of the public, and the history of reception, mostly summarizing previous research, but not establishing much new ground.

A Few Comments on the Problem of Translating Late Medieval German Verse Narratives

Insofar as Kaufringer followed the practice observed by most of his contemporaries, rendering all of his texts in verse form with a specific rhyming scheme, he was often forced to use an odd syntactic structure, allowing repetitions to enter his text, or saying the same thing twice in different words or in somewhat different syntactic contexts. This required for the English translation at times to reverse the sentences, to eliminate duplications, or to 'translate' the metaphorical statements in order to make sense out of them in the new linguistic context. Otherwise, I have stayed as close to the original as possible and have tried to render it into an idiomatically correct English. At times, however, that was simply not quite realistic because otherwise I would not have translated but recreated the text. The reader can follow the narrative by means of the verse references (every five verses). Only a few times did I have to move text around greatly in order to maintain the required English grammatical structure. This means that in a few cases the verse number does not coincide exactly with the actual original text because of syntactical constraints.

Often Kaufringer used filler words for the rhyming scheme, and I tried as best as possible to render these as well without making the text repetitive or meaningless—there are countless adverbial phrases meaning "right away," or "immediately," that were added for rhyming purposes only. It often proved to be reasonable to eliminate those redundant words, especially if they did not carry significant meaning.

Since Kaufringer employed an East Swabian dialect, it was occasionally difficult to determine the exact meaning, since the standard dictionaries of Middle High German do not always offer the needed explanation. I have regularly relied on the famous Lexer, the BMZ (Benecke, Müller, Zarnke), and then also on a variety of other dictionaries for various German dialects, available online at the *Wörterbuchnetz* operated and maintained by the Trier Center for Digital Humanities: http://woerterbuchnetz.de/cgi-bin/WBNetz/startGlobalSearch. tcl?stichwort=mede (last accessed on Sept. 5, 2014).

One difficulty with Kaufringer's text is that his language no longer reflects traditional Middle High German; instead linguistically the poet is already situated at the point of transition toward Early New High German. In addition, considering his reliance on numerous dialectical phrases, in my translation I occasionally encountered some hard problems that I could solve only through creative solutions. Interestingly, the *Elsässisches Wörterbuch* offered solutions more often than I would have expected, even though late medieval Alsatian is far away from Swabian.

The present book is a translation, and it does not substitute for the original text. The reader is thus strongly advised to pick up Kaufringer's original verse narratives, to place them next to the translation, and to enjoy his works in both versions. Mostly, however, I believe that this English translation will make his texts particularly accessible especially to those who do not read or study Middle High German literature, yet would like to become familiar with some of the most important early fifteenth-century literature from German-speaking lands. Occasionally, I have added in square brackets the literal meaning of a passage, while the translation itself presents a more idiomatically correct one, or an alternative term that captures, as far as I can tell, the original meaning better. Or I give an explanation of what the term might really mean, as I had to translate it in accordance with what the author says. At times I had to change the tenses in the original to remain consistent in the overall syntactical structure of a whole passage, which is standard practice in current translation efforts.[45] In numerous footnotes I have explained in more detail the textual problem or added short explanations of the content. But expansive remarks I have reserved for the endnotes.

Altogether, I hope I have rendered Kaufringer's works as appropriately as possible into modern English, thus making him accessible and attractive once again. His *mæren* prove to be another good example why we in the twenty-first century still, or once again, find medieval literature so fascinating, intriguing, and productive for us as modern readers. We do not have to agree with all the opinions voiced in Kaufringer's work, but many of his tales certainly offer remarkable perspectives and examples of human life that are of timeless value.

To illustrate this volume, I have included a number of photos showing us landmarks of the town of Landsberg, and then a selection of typical urban scenes in a variety of European cities within their medieval context.

---

[45] See, for instance, the comments by Donald Maddox and Sara Sturm-Maddox on their approach to the translation of Jean d'Arras's *Melusine*, 2012, 14–16.

HEINRICH KAUFRINGER'S
VERSE NARRATIVES

No. 1: *The Hermit and the Angel*

God does so many miracles that no one can ever count them all, as we learn clearly in Scripture: "mirabilis deus in sanctis suis."[1] This means: "God is full of wonders (5) in His manifold works of miracles." The human mind cannot grasp the wonders that God works, and no one can ever grasp it all. I have learned this from one person (10) who was truly a saintly brother and served God so anxiously for twelve years living in a forest that God had sent him heavenly food.

He, about whom I talked above (15), felt the desire one day to learn about the miracles that God works. He made up his mind to find out about them to the fullest possible extent. He quickly embarked on a journey (20) and intended to traverse the whole world. A beautiful and attractive angel came to him in the figure of a pilgrim. He said: "Greetings to you in the name of God, you old brother! Tell me, where do you want to go?" (25)[2] The hermit said: "All my intentions are directed toward the goal of how I could learn about God's miracles, which happen everywhere; there are many that are unaccountable for (30). I want to understand what they are; that is my desire." The angel said: "Then I beg you to allow me to be your fellow (35), and you will do me a great favor with that." The brother said: "If you want to give me good company, as I will do to you, I would be happy to be your fellow." They pledged companionship to each other (40) without fail as good brothers do to each other.

They walked until the sun began to set and the day turned to evening. When they reached a town, (45) they were kindly welcomed by a virtuous and wealthy burger [i.e., inn keeper]. He said to them humbly: "If you want to rest here in the name of God, then please accept my invitation. (50) I will give you a comfortable rest for the entire night until the early morning." They were very pleased when they heard his words und entered the inn. There they found enough room for themselves. (55) The inn keeper happily served them a meal and good wine well selected, which satisfied their hunger, making them forget their exhaustion.

Now, this good man (60) had an honorable and beautiful wife who was a complete delight for his heart. God had granted them a delightful child. The inn keeper, his wife, and the servants gave complete attention (65) to this lovely child

---

[1] Psalms 67:36: God is wonderful in his saints. There are many biblical references in Kaufringer's text, which I have not identified specifically, leaving this for future research.

[2] Significantly, the hermit does not recognize that the pilgrim is, in reality, an angel. He will realize that only at the very end.

and they cared about nothing else. They exerted themselves day and night to in-sure the child's well-being. The inn-keeper said to the two men: (70) "My guests, if you want to go to sleep, then let me know this. Whatever you have consumed here, you will have received through God [free of charge]." They thanked him very much for his kind words (75) and followed his advice, immediately going to bed. The guests were well cared for, both with respect to their bodily needs and their goods, just as an honorable host should do (80) who takes good care of his guests.

When dawn began and it turned light, the two pilgrims did not linger and prepared themselves for their continued journey. (85) [At that point] the wet nurse, in the early morning, carried the tender child into the living room. Hon-estly, I must say it shone forth bright as the moon, it was beautiful and attrac-tive. (90) It slept quietly in the manger. Then, the wet nurse left the room, left the child behind, and did some work in the house that called for her attention. (95) The angel sat down next to the child and said to his fellow: "Look at this beautiful child; it is so sweet and delightful." He took a pillow in his hand (100) and put it on the child's mouth. Then he sat on it right away and suffocated the child. That was a great pain for the hermit brother, but he could not prevent it (105). He said: "Truly, you are an evil person, why did you commit the murder of this praiseworthy child, and why did you do that to his virtuous father who has given us food and drink [wine] (110) and has treated us so well? You have done an abominable deed. I clearly observe in this situation that benefaction is wasted to you. He who pays back a good deed with an evil deed (115) is truly a devil-ish person. You might well be the child of the devil, whom all evil people obey."

The angel said: "Now be quiet! I have carried out my own intention (120), since I have not come here to care about anyone's opinion." The brother thought to himself: "How do I get away from here before people hear rumors about the murder that has been done to this child?" (125) Straightaway he left the house and the city, but the angel ran quickly after him because he wanted to go on a pilgrimage only with him. That, however, displeased the brother mightily, (130) but he could not do anything against it, so he had to let him come along.

In the evening they came to a large and great city, and found the house of an honorable man. (135) They stayed there without experiencing any problem. The inn-keeper was virtuous and wealthy. He owned a chalice that was expertly embossed with gold and silver. Honestly, I must tell you, (140) it was certainly worth twelve marks. He honored his guests by serving drinks in it. He placed it in front of them on the table. He provided them with venison and fish and every other imaginable food item in large quantities. (145) His guest left him and felt very well filled and satisfied. He also provided them with good sleeping quarters and gave them some travel money.

When dawn came, the angel did another amazing thing, (150) as I tell you. Secretly, in the morning, when they left, the angel stole the valuable chalice, cov-ered with silver and gold in good measure. (155) His brother, the holy man, had turned to his prayer while the angel committed the theft. When they were on their way, the angel said: "I have secretly taken (160) the valuable chalice from the inn keeper. I took it away with me this morning." He pulled it out of his bag. The brother said: "You evil dragon, you are filled so much with disloyalty; (165) the inn keeper has provided us with so much hospitality and yet you took away from him his property. Truly, I tell you, I never want to be your companion again; I cannot reach my goal with you. (170) If I were to stay with you for a long time, we both might well be hanged something I have never aimed for." The angel responded: "You foolish man, if you want to explore the world, (175) you will have to witness much greater wonders than those that I have done so far. Let us have high spirits and move forward. Truly, get this into your head." (180)

The brother sat down, he wanted to move neither forward nor backward together with the angel, but the latter refused to leave him, because he always wanted to stay with him. They fought over this (185) until it became night, when they caught sight of a beautiful city, about a mile away. They strove to reach it with haste (190) and would have liked to enter it, yet they had to stay outside because it had become very late [and the city gates were locked]. Outside of the city wall they found a house with a vile hospitality (195): the guests experienced few favors. An evil and low-minded inn-keeper lived there, who liked to charge much and offered very little in return. Many experienced suffering there. (200)

Then night set in. The two pilgrims heard loud noise all over the house, created by a multitude of ruffians engaged in all kinds of games, (205) uttering curses and many other bad words. The two pilgrims entered the dangerous house, only to realize that finding good space was difficult. They would have liked to sit down, but the benches were occupied (210) by evil characters and knaves from Hungary, Bohemia, and Poland who were lying and sitting on them. The two brothers did not eat or drink anything there and had a miserable time (215) until it became light again the next day. They wanted to depart immediately, but the inn keeper said to the two: "You must pay for the time you spent here sleeping, before you leave from here, (220) and for everything you have consumed in my place, or I will not allow you to continue your travel." The brother said: "But we have neither eaten nor drunk anything here, since no one was willing to give us anything. (225) We will pay you for the night only grudgingly because of the hard beds, which hardly had any feathers." The angel said: "Not that way, dear brother! We are not in an evil house here (230). The inn keeper is an honorable man. He shall have the richly ornamented chalice, as I pledge on my honor." He took it out of his bag and handed it over to the inn-keeper (235). The brother's face turned pale because of this amazing turn of events. He did not dare to speak up against the companion's decision. The innkeeper gave them his great thanks. Then they departed from there. (240)

When they walking along, the brother said: "On the highways that I have used and in rough fields I have wanted to experience God's wonders.[3] But now I have been assigned (245) by the devil an evil companion, the devil's own servant, who is doing the devil's work all the time.[4] It would have been better if I had stayed home and spent my time in the service of God, (250) as I have done for many years, instead of witnessing the deeds of the evil devil who has sent you here to this land." The angel said: "You are not wise; (255) you are old and white-haired. If anyone does something against you, you still are supposed to be good and forgive the other his wrong doing. This must happen according to God's will. (260) If you do not protest against it, your salvation will be increasingly secured." The brother said: "This confirms to me that you are void of virtue and in sync with the devil, (265) because if anyone looks at you in a friendly manner and shares what he has with you, you strike back against all custom by repaying it with evilness and heart rendering pain. (270) You suffocated the child of the one man; from the other man you secretly took his drinking cup [chalice] and handed it over to another man who has never done anything good to you and me or anyone else in the world (275). That is [rightfully] called fulfilling the devil's command."

Once he had finished speaking, they had reached a river on which many ships traveled. A bridge crossed the river (280) leading to a city. The brother stepped onto the bridge, and the angel did the same. They wanted to enter city right away. They needed to find food there (285) because the evil inn keeper had not provided them with good provisions, as you have heard before. When they had reached the middle of the bridge and were on top of the river, the good angel turned around. (290) He saw a man come running and rushing up to them. The angel said: "What makes this man hurry? Let us wait and stand here until we have learned fully (295) what has happened [recently] in his life." When he got to them, the angel grabbed him at his arms and pushed him immediately off the bridge down into the water. (300) In the depth of the river he faced bitter death.

The brother yelled out loudly: "Help, why is God asleep that he does not take revenge on you (305) for the evil deeds, of which you commit so many? Indeed, I no longer want to walk with you, neither here nor there." The angel said: "You pledged to be my companion, as I did to you, (310) and if you no longer want to be my companion, then call me quits of my loyalty." The brother said: "Your loyalty is miniscule; be free of it and go away, so that I can complete my pilgrimage. (315) I want to go to the end of the world." The angel said: "Now, pay attention, I want to make you understand who I am and why I came to provide you with some instruction: (320) I am an angel sent by God."

---

[3] He uses present tense, but the present perfect tense seems to make more sense in this context since he reflects back upon his experiences up to that point.

[4] In the original it says "wunder," but the hermit can only mean the very opposite to God's "wonders," hence simply "works."

Immediately his worldly shape disappeared, and the brother saw standing in front of him a beautiful and well-shaped angel in his divine glory. (325) The brother felt great heart-aches that he had maligned him so badly all the time with his disparaging words. He fell on his knees and said: "Have mercy, lord, with me here! (330) Do not make me suffer for having treated you badly with ignorant words; I beg you for that, dear lord, I ask you humbly."

The angel truly said: (335) "The miracles and the sorrowful deeds caused by me that you witnessed have happened for your sake." The brother said: "Now let me know, you messenger from God, if you are so kind, (340) why did you kill the child, which has turned the father and his servants into our enemies."[5] The angel answered him right away: "That inn keeper and his wife (345) suffered from great sorrow and pain because they did not have a child. They begged God every night and day to grant them a child. (350) Everything they desired in their heart God gave them. All their sorrow was taken away. Although the woman was infertile, she became pregnant after all (355) against the rules of nature. Soon enough God gave them that child. From then on they strove more for profit than they had ever done before. They loved to do nothing more (360) than to spoil the child [with the money]. They completely forgot about God and would have been lost for all eternity, if I had not turned my wrath against the child (365) and imposed[6] on it a painful death. Now they can be unified with God because they obey His laws [again]."

The brother said: "Now tell me more, holy angel in the service of God, (370) why did you steal the valuable drinking vessel from the inn keeper who housed us so well and who even provided us with a good place to stay overnight for little money? You gave the very same drinking vessel (375) to the inn keeper who had few virtues and who acted badly against us in an evil fashion. Let me understand that without delay." The shining angel said in reply: "I tell you in truth, (380) the man who had owned that chalice was pious and good; he had acquired all his possessions legitimately without any evil deception except for the ornamented chalice. (385) It had been brought to his house and given to him in bribery as a reward for treason. He had received and then kept the chalice, which expelled him from eternal life and chased him away from it. (390)[7] Now he owns all his property according to God's will because all his possessions are good and pure. He, however, to whom I gave the chalice, possessed few proper goods, owned little that he had acquired properly, whether small or large, (395) and it all served him just as he pleased him. He gained his wealth against the law of God, as many people nowadays do. This inn keeper now gains some joy from the drinking cup

---

[5] The verb "erputten" in the original does not seem to exist in the relevant dictionaries, but the context implies that Kaufringer intended to use the cognate "erbôsen," "to get angry with," or "to hate."

[6] The term "gesprengen" means "to attack," or "to jump at."

[7] In order to make sense out of this sentence, I had to reverse the entire grammatical structure.

View from the harbor, the town of Krk, Croatia

that I gave him (400) and has more of the happiness of heaven here on earth [as he believes] because in the afterlife he will be condemned for eternity and will be lost, suffering pain forever."

The brother said: "Now tell me, (405) what was your heart's intention when you pushed that good man into deep water, in which he drowned? Teach me that right away." (410) The angel responded: "His life was like this: he was a wild usurer and had caused many people, who were free of all guilt, great trouble. (415) Now he wanted to gain God's grace quickly. Filled with repentance he came from the forest and arrived here. He wanted to confess and receive his penance (420) from the priest in the city. When he approached me, I immediately recognized that he would not be able to preserve this good life [his newly found religious devotion]. (425) He would [as I recognized] commit even more evil deeds and would be lost to sinfulness. I wanted to preserve his soul, while he was still filled with good intentions. I pushed him without any hatred (430) off the bridge into the deep water, so that he would lose his life. His soul is now in God's realm and will stay there forever. Therefore, my dear brother, (435) return to your cell, because all the wonders that God does happen only for good purposes. No longer question anything and follow my teachings, (440) which will give you protection for ever."

Having finished speaking the angel turned to God and disappeared. The brother went home to his cell (445) and did as the angel had taught him. He completed his life dedicated to God and was protected by the throng of angels.

No. 2: *The Converted Jew*

When Christianity rose and the Jewish faith quickly dissipated and the Christian community grew, many infidels converted, (5) who were all encouraged in their heart to stand by Christ and to let go the false faith. At those times there was a Jew who hated Christianity. (10) No one could convince him that he should let go of his error and accept the Christian faith. Therefore he was openly hated by everyone (15) because he did not follow the right religion. They began to chase him away; he could not stay anywhere without facing opposition, and this happened wherever he went. He was a disgrace to everyone (20) because he did not want to be a Christian. For that reason he suffered much pain.

One day he came to a city where he very much wanted to stay. He had many friends there (25) to whom he was closely attached. But they had all converted and accepted the Christian faith. When they noticed that he was openly a Jew (30) and despised the Christian faith, they denied him any housing; no one wanted to offer him lodging, and these were all those who used to be his friends, since they no longer wanted to see him. (35) He went back and forth, walked up and down all streets in the city, but wherever he asked for a welcome, no one wanted to let him in. He was thus forced to spend the night (40) in the Jewish synagogue. The building where they had once gone on a regular basis was now nothing more than a ruin, because the entire city had accepted (45) the Christian faith. No one paid attention to the synagogue any more. Before all the Jews had held it in great respect; it had been their cherished synagogue. (50)

The sorrowful foreigner went there, because he needed a place to rest for the night. He laid there in the forlorn house, when he had a horrifying experience, which almost made him lose his mind. (55) He remembered that the good Christian community was well cared for and protected from all kinds of misfortune by the sign of the cross. (60) He would have liked to protect himself with it [as well], but he was so firm in his own faith that he suffered great pain from his fear before he submitted himself (65) to bear the yoke of the Holy Cross.

When it turned midnight, the Jew heard loud noises and a terrifying sound. Lucifer, the evil devil (70) and three sinister multitudes of his servants arrived in that synagogue. He carried on his head (75) a valuable and finely wrought crown and on his arm three more crowns. His servants stood in front of him, divided into three groups. He was seated powerfully (80) on a throne. Quickly he demanded that the captain of the first army appear before him, who knelt in front of him. Lucifer said to him: (85) "What kinds of wars and suffering have you

caused in the world with your army?" The devil servant answered him as follows:
"Lord, I have sent out to the world (90) with the help of my soldiers a problem
that caused two major lords developed great envy and enmity for each other; now
six thousand people are buried who have been slain. (95) This massive murder I
and my subjects have caused." "You will receive my thanks," said Lucifer thereupon: "Let me also know, (100) how long it took you to plan this evil deed until it
was completed." The devil answered him thereupon: "Only within twenty weeks,
no longer (105) the army of my companions and myself accomplished this task
well." As a reward Lucifer placed one of the crowns on his head, which pleased
the devil mightily. (110)

Then Lucifer called upon the captain of the other army, who arrived immediately and also knelt before him. Lucifer addressed him as follows: "How did
you do carry out your service for me, (115) together with your army? I want to
bestow a reward upon you, so let me know. Have you torn someone away from
God who now follows my law?" (120) The devil answered: "Yes, dear lord. There
is a hermit far away, living in a large forest. He led a very pure life for a long time.
(125) For years I pursued him to fill him with envy. I and the entire army have
convinced him, since we never gave him a break, (130) to sleep with a beautiful
woman, just as we advised him to do, and to be with her in an unchaste manner. We gained both the body and the soul of that good man. (135) God has now
abandoned him."

Lucifer was very pleased with those words. He took a crown from his arm
and placed it on his captain's head. He said: "Because you have robbed (140) eternal life from that hermit, I want to give you as a reward the rank of king, ruling
over your companions." The devil was very happy about that. (145)

Now the captain of the third army was ready to report. Lucifer urged him
to tell him how he had served him. (150) The captain also knelt down and said:
"I have truly suffered badly with the pope for more than seven years; now I have
succeeded in planting the idea (155) to pursue an unchaste life in his mind. I in-
sinuated this to him many times. Now he has started an affair with an attractive
woman (160), whom he kissed on her lips. He also touched her breast immediately, full of lust. It will take no more than half a year until I and my servants
(165) convince him to sleep with her [enjoy her body] and make her to his wife
[concubine]."[1] Lucifer was mightily pleased with these words. He took a crown
from his arm (170), and placed it on the captain's head and exuberantly thanked
him for his service. He said: "Do not ever rest until the pope has fallen (175) into
sinfulness through his lack of chastity and his erotic desires; then I will give you
as an award the coronet from my head, with which you will be crowned indeed. I
will then concede my power to you, (180) once you have accomplished your task."

---

[1] Kaufringer uses the word "eeweib" (wife), but the pope would never have been able
to marry; hence the more appropriate word seems to be "concubine."

The Jew, who was a complete stranger to that company, was lying there in the synagogue, filled with fear and great horror. He saw and heard those events (185) and witnessed many terrifying scenes. Then his anxiety grew so much that he protected his body with the sign of Christianity. He made the sign of the Holy Cross (190) and blessed himself so that the devils could not hurt him, not even by the breadth of a small hair. When the devils noticed the cross, they felt great pain. (195) "Who might that be here among us?" they all yelled. Making much noise, they found the Jew lying in the synagogue. But no one dared to approach (200) the stranger. They began to flee from him and said altogether, filled with hatred: "Here lies a miserable barrel covered with a crucifix (205). No one at this moment can do any damage to him." They immediately fled from the synagogue, and not one of them stayed behind.

The Jew spent the night there (210) with great discomfort until the early morning dawned. When the day had begun, the Jew ended his sleep. He got up and left the place. (215) Great doubt filled him regarding his own faith. He greatly liked the cross, the sign of Christianity, which had protected him from suffering (220) and from the devil's evil nature. He turned his mind immediately to the question how he could approach the pope in order to receive the Christian faith from him, along with Christian baptism (225). He felt a strong urge to go to Rome.

When he got to the pope, he took him aside and knelt down before him. He said: "My dear father, (230) I have been called a Jew until now, therefore I want to go to confession. I want to embrace the Christian faith. I will tell you what I have to confess, (235) from deep at the bottom of my heart."

The pope helped him. The Jew told him everything he had ever done before. He also revealed to the pope (240) what his life had been like. The devils would have done even worse to him had he not taken care of his own life with the blessing of the Holy Cross. He also warned the pope himself (245) to keep body and soul away from the delightful woman, whom he had seduced and kissed in a very seductive manner, advising him that he should not allow love (250) to overpower him, as the Jew had heard the evil devil announced.[2] Otherwise it would hurt his soul badly and impose eternal death [condemnation] on him. (255)

When the pope realized that he had told him the truth, he immediately eschewed the pretty woman [from then on] and removed all thoughts about her from his heart so that he could protect himself well (260) from the suffering in hell, and instead gain a throne in heaven.

Right away the pope baptized the Jew, who learned everything about the Christian faith. He turned into a truly saintly man, (265) whom the pope liked so much that he employed him at his court where he stayed until the end of his life and then was able to join the heavenly host. (270)

---

[2] Kaufringer uses the noun "clag" — "complaint," but the devil had only announced gleefully that he was about to overpower the pope.

Everyone should learn from this that nothing is as useful to gain salvation of the pure soul and access to heaven than to be concerned (275) always and consistently with the sign of the Holy Cross. Then no evil spirit can ever hurt him or cheat him. If a person is strong (280) enough to withstand sinfulness,[3] then the devil's advice cannot cause him any harm. The devil pulls us down at day and night with his wrong teachings (285) and sneaks behind us without making any sound. As a protection God has given us the sign of the Holy Cross, with which God will protect us wherever we travel on horseback or otherwise (290), now and forever. May the Holy Christ help us!

---

[3] Here and throughout I always try to avoid a gender bias, referring to s/he, or him/her if possible, but at times this becomes too clumsy stylistically, so the masculine pronoun always includes, when generically used, the female as well.

No. 3: *The Peasant Who Was [Falsely] Accused*

No one causes more sorrow for people than corrupt judges and also some clerics. The person who has to deal with them is in great need of good luck (5) if he wants to avoid major problems. When they form an alliance or when they plot together (I mean the judge and the smart priest), then the person of whom they are envious (10) must take great care to act precisely according to the law. If he kills only one chicken by accident, he must pay with four horses as a penance, or face a long-lasting feud with them. It might eventually result (15) that they show him mercy and demand that he give them a fully-grown oxen for a penance.[1] In that way he pays for that one chicken. On top of it he must do one more thing: (20) he must thank them immediately that they had treated him so kindly. It often and repeatedly happens that one ends up in prison who is virtuous and does evil ends up in prison. (25) They punish him physically and materially, which is arranged by means of a judgment.

Now, I think that a person who has not done anything wrong should not let himself be frightened. (30) He should, rather, risk experiencing his doom right away at the hands of knights and their servants or find justice at his trial, as a peasant once did (35) who enjoyed all the unnecessary public esteem and material wealth. He lived in a good village, was virtuous, and he did not desire what did not belong to him. He also did not lend money to anyone (40) because of his miserliness which was so great that no one enjoyed any of his goods, neither the priest nor the judge. His nature was kind, that, if anyone harbored evil intentions against him, (45) he knew how to defend himself at all times with good manners and wisdom. He was also loath to hold back what he was obliged to give. (50) He gave his seven offerings[2] and paid his tithe without grumbling. Otherwise, l no one else profited from his goods.

I tell you truly that the priest hated him for this. (55) He thought to himself: "How do I achieve my goal of making of this peasant the people's laughing stock, whose wealth neither the world nor God can enjoy? Indeed, I must cause him some harm." He asked the judge (60) to visit him in his grand house. They both enjoyed each other's company. The priest began to speak: "Judge, let me tell you, there is a peasant in my parish (65) who wants to be his own lord and who respects neither you nor me very much. He owns much money. If you want to help

---

[1] The narrator clearly means this in an ironic fashion.
[2] Special offerings on seven major Church holidays.

me to bring it about, I will not grant him any respite [from my attacks]: (70) his power must be crushed, and he must be subjected by us. He is not a good Christian, a fact which I will quickly demonstrate, and you will profit from that, (75) to tell the truth." He pointed out that peasant to him. The judge was very pleased by these words, since he enjoyed gaining wealth, as every judge does [today]. (80) He said: "In fact, this peasant always seems to be angry; I have been upset about him for a long time and have never profited from him not even by the breadth of a hair. (85) It has been ten years now that I have been an elected as a judge here yet I have never gotten the smallest amount of money from him."

The judge and the priest, both filled with hatred, mutually swore an oath (90) to help each other to cause the peasant some harm. Seven days later a strong thunderstorm occurred, smashing, hitting the land. (95) The priest offered prayers against the terrible weather in his parish. God demonstrated with His power that He was all their lord. The heavy rain destroyed (100) in that community all the good and excellent crop; nothing was spared. As a consequence of this misery the people voiced great lamentations (105) both day and night, because the heavy thunderstorm threatened their lives. Then the peasant (110) whom the priest hated, said publicly, when he heard the people's laments: "Truly, you are all fools to lament at this time. It was, believe me, good weather after all. (115) No one will have to suffer or experience pain, that's what I am telling you, because God Himself has done that to us."

No one liked to hear those words, I have to admit. (120) When the priest noticed this, he thought to himself: "Now I have some evidence at hand to move against this peasant because he voiced those mean words quite seriously, not as a joke. (125) We can now claim that he is not a good Christian." He was very happy that he was holding a trump card against the good man (130), with which he could cause him pain; his heart did not desire for anything else.

Not long thereafter the priest was reading mass on a high feast day. (135) The peasant was performing his own work on the sacred cemetery. He intended to complete the work of mowing all sixty meadows. (140) He openly enjoyed his work. At that moment the priest arrived at the altar from his prayer. He turned around and noticed it all. He let his envy, (145) which swelled in his heart, come forward. Filled with wrath he spoke up: "Now let me tell you all that I have, here in my parish, a truly evil-doing man, (150) who cares nothing about the church service. He gives little honor to God and the world. You can easily recognize him, but I do not want to mention his name. He is talking loudly (155) and would not think twice about making a fool outside in the cemetery in front of the holy altar. I tell you frankly (160) that he is not a good Christian. I will no longer spare him: if he does not improve quickly, I will identify him openly and expose him to the mockery of the world; (165) afterward he will have to do penance to God." After he had spoken, everyone looked at each other amidst the crowd attending mass. Soon the people began to move, (170) everyone stepping in front of the other trying to exit through the church door. Outside they wanted to see to whom the words applied. There they found the peasant, . (175) He had not abandoned any of his self-confidence, to the contrary. They recognized that he was the one whom the priest had criticized.

The peasant was quickly informed (180) by those who meant well by him what the angry priest had said about him, and that he was [allegedly] the public enemy of the entire village. (185) He had a heavy heart thereupon. He thought to himself: "What is going on here? Am I indeed so evil and weak that I am called a bad Christian? God Himself knows (190) that I am innocent in that regard." He made up his mind not to be intimidated. Perhaps the priest had spoken those words about another person, not about himself. (195) He also determined that, since the priest had not mentioned anyone by name, he himself could not have been insulted [meant], so he kept quiet and did not feel bothered. (200)

Afterwards, upon a Sunday, when everyone had gathered for holy mass, the priest thought: "I hate this peasant very much; (205) I must chastise him today if he does not correct himself and submit to." When he had announced the conclusion of mass, while still in the pulpit and his sermon about to end, (210) he asked the people to remain standing quietly and said: "Now take note, my dear children, everyone who is here in church! As I told you before, (215) there is one among my flock who challenges his own Christian values; he does not care about God and the world. Indeed, he is an evil Christian. I tell you honestly, (220) he must be a displeasure to God and an enemy to the whole world." Now, the priest held a big rock in his hand, as he stood above the people. He said: "I do not dare to name (225) this truly wicked person, but I will throw this rock at him." He turned toward the peasant when he spied him in the crowd. He acted as if he wanted to throw (230) the heavy rock at him. The peasant bent down and threw himself quickly to the ground. Although the stone never left the hand of the angry priest, (235) the judge apprehended the peasant when he came out of the church. He took him away as a prisoner. He called him a vile heretic (240) about to lose his life because he had admitted his guilt in the church in front of the entire congregation, when he had ducked away from the stone, although he had never been hit by it. (245) He had exposed himself at that moment.

When the peasant was imprisoned, his friends did not hesitate to visit him immediately, and many others as well. (250) They all deplored his situation. He responded without showing any fear: "I am not aware of any fault that I might have committed against the church or secular laws. (255) The priest is maligning me. I will contradict everything that he charges me with, whatever the outcome might be; it will not worry me."

Now the priest had also arrived (260) at the house with his companions. He heard the peasant's words as well. He said: "I will prove that you are void of virtues. You are not striving toward heaven. (265) You much more prefer temporary goods over God. That is sinfulness and a terrible matter. Of course, it is my obligation to protect you from hell (270) and to help you to get to heaven, but that is the limit of my duties toward my flock." The peasant said: "Leave me alone with your threats [penalty] and your reprimands. (275) I'll protect myself from hell. I am also confident of getting to heaven, surely without your help, since I have in my house both heaven and hell [the pain of hell]." (280)

The priest said: "Now I clearly hear that you are filled with a false faith and that you are truly an evil Christian, because you believe that both hell and heaven exist in your house. (285) My lords, note altogether the words that he has uttered, since they contradict the [true] faith. If he denies later having uttered those words, I can prove the opposite through your testimony." (290) The peasant responded: "Truly, I am not going to deny what I just said. No harm will come to me because of those words; I can well prove that I spoke the truth." The priest answered: "Soon the day will come when you will have to figure out (295) how to safeguard your life by means of your intelligence, which is low. You are blind with open eyes. You will still be forced to turn away from your foolish attitude! I will protect you from the judge (300) and his punishment, if you follow my teaching." The peasant said to the priest: "I have nothing to negotiate with you or the judge. (305) You have brought great suffering upon me without any legitimate reason. I do not need to beg for the judge's mercy just because I am imprisoned here. Your wisdom and your mind (310) will help me little. I have a good horse at home that has more smarts than you. How would you thus be able to advise me?" (315)

The priest said: "Listen, my companions, he has insulted me, claiming that his horse is more intelligent than I; that is unbelievable. How could it be (320) that he is a good Christian, filled with such foolishness? Recently he even stated, without any qualms, that when the thunderstorm caused us so much damage, destroying all the crops in our fields, (325) that the weather had been good. He has no faith who makes such comments publicly." The peasant said: "You are right, (330) I am not denying that I said that. I made my comments in public, and I can support their truth indeed, when I am properly asked to do so." The priest said: "You have done enough (335) damage and foolishness. I will ride to the court of my lord, the bishop; I will raise my complaints about you to him. The three charges are enough (340) to affirm that you are blind in your faith." The peasant said: "I desire nothing more than to defend myself before the lord bishop and his wise council (345) for the alleged misdeeds and thus rejoice in my innocence."

The judge then released the peasant from the prison temporarily until the time when the case would be decided (350) on the condition, as the peasant community pledged, that the accused would submit himself again and return to the judge's court (355) into the same prison.

The priest did not linger any longer, prepared for his journey, and quickly went on horseback to the court of his lord, the bishop. (360) He said: "Lord, please listen to me! I have to tell Your Grace that there is a peasant in my parish who refuses to be a good Christian. (365) A bad thunderstorm caused much damage in my parish. The downpour left nothing behind [of the crop], as it destroyed everything we could harvest for this (370) and following years. Thereupon that one peasant said maliciously that it was good weather. Moreover, there are two further grave charges against him. (375) He publicly said that he has in his house both heaven and the terror of hell. (380) When I was about to punish him, he said that I am lacking in wisdom; his horse would be much wiser than me. Lord, he causes me great pain with those words because it is against [Christian] faith (385) and contradicts what we call a good Christian."

The bishop, when he had listened to his words said in response: "This is a strange account. He is truly a heretic (390) who dares to say such things, and he is also a fool. I will not let him go unpunished, if he makes such comments."

The priest went home again, (395) and the peasant no longer lingered in the village. He soon went to the court, filled with joy, without any worries. He had no concern because he had good supporters. (400) He took a seat in the council of canons. Truly, I want to tell you, his lords were all positively inclined toward him, since he served them by giving them many rich gifts. When he had arrived there, (405) the bishop noticed him and said: "Come here, you foul peasant! How dare you to be so evil and bitter! Your priest has raised serious charges against you, saying that you do not want to follow his teachings. (410)

When the thunderstorm causes damage to your [village], you call it good weather. You claim to have heaven and the pain of hell in your home. Moreover, you have said your horse has more intelligence (415) than the priest. If you really make such statements, then you are not following the right path as prescribed by the [Christian] faith." He responded: "Lord, this is all as I have said. Your honor, without being forced to do so, (420) I will openly demonstrate this in front of your council, as it behooves me. The bishop said: "Now tell me right away (425), how is it possible that you have the power to possess hell and heaven? That is truly impossible. Give me proof of it right away, or you will reveal that you are an evil Christian." (430)

The peasant answered: "Dear Lord, the holding I received from you is not far from here. Please come with your councilors and your lawyers to my farm (435) and look at the conditions there. It will provide you with some entertainment. There you will hear and truly see how I can provide evidence for my claim, (440) because I want to have justice." The bishop replied in a good mood: "Truly, that will be. On the next Sunday we will visit your home, (445) and make sure that we will be regaled with wine. Under those circumstances, we will come quickly. He who is proven wrong will have to pay for it."

With [the bishop's] permission the peasant went home. He did as his lord had told him (450). He ordered wine and enough food. He butchered a cow for the kitchen, and arranged everything properly, as is expected when one serves his lord. The bishop did (455) as he had told the peasant, arriving early on Sunday morning with all of his councilmen. Many wise people were present. The smart peasant happily served (460) excellent wine and food. They all had a good time and were satisfied, enjoying themselves very much. After the meal, when the tables were removed, the priest also arrived (465) with the judge, who were [the peasant's] opponents and hoped to achieve great success. But they became the butt of the joke, as you will soon learn. (470)

The bishop addressed the priest: "Let us know your complaints and raise your charges about what the peasant has done to you." The priest immediately answered: (475) "Lord, I will let you know. The peasant has made three danger-ous statements,[3] which are very much opposed to the holy Christian faith. The thunderstorm has caused us great damage in our fields (480). Indeed, it did not leave anything for us and struck everything down into the soil, so that there will not be any crop, which we need.[4] (485) The peasant said without any concern and filled with arrogance that the weather had been good here."

In response the peasant said: "Lord, that is true. I am saying this openly (490) that it was good weather. God brought it upon us only for our own good because He never does anything evil. He reminded us thereby (495) to let go of our evil behavior and our sinfulness. We have to accept our penance through this heavy thunderstorm. If we behaved otherwise (500) and observed God's com-mands and rejected the mockery of God by sins both privately and publicly, with words and also with deeds, pushing sin away, (505) then we would never experi-ence from God such horror and pain, as my heart is telling me."

The bishop said to the priest: "The peasant ought not to suffer any punish-ment (510) for that 'misdeed.' He has not spoken badly. He can stand proudly by those words quite well, to tell you the truth. Now tell me," said the lord bishop (515), "what else has the peasant said that contradicts the faith?" he priest an-swered immediately: "Dear Lord, I will do that gladly. The peasant refuses to re-ceive [the proper] teaching (520) about how to find the right way to heaven. He also does not care about how to protect himself from hell. He said openly that he has in his house (525) both heaven and the suffering of hell. When I wanted to correct him with my teaching,[5] in which I am an expert, he obstructed my teach-ing by saying that his horse is wiser than me. (530) Lord, considering all that, I realize that he does not hold the right faith."

The peasant replied: "My dear lord, the priest has caused me great sorrow and pain without any fault on my part. (535) I pronounce by God's grace that I am a good Christian and that I have nothing else on my mind but good Christian faith. Truly, I am fully justified in claiming (540) that I have the suffering of hell and the heavenly kingdom in my house." He asked the bishop to come with him, along with his servants who had been invited to his house. (545) He led them to a dark room in the back of his house, where his mother was lying in bed. She had been confined to bed for about thirty-two years. (550) A very foul smell was in that room and could be noticed both day and night without end. The peasant

---

[3] The word "artickel" could be rendered as "articles of faith," but I simplify here be-cause the priest only charges him of some heretical comments.

[4] Literally: "which would be of good use for us."

[5] The original has present tense here, but the priest refers to past events.

said: "Here is hell and heaven. You know this for certain because if I treat my mother well (555) I will have guaranteed access to heaven. If I were not doing that, I would become part of the hellish throng."

The lords looked at each other [full of surprise]. The good bishop then spoke (560): "It seems to me that the peasant is a truly just person." One of the lawyers said without delay: "Lord, it is written [in the Bible] that God grants a long life to that person who honors his father and mother well [fourth commandment]; (565) for that he will gain eternal reward. [On the other hand], the person who treats his father and mother badly wastes all his good deeds and will end up in the fire of hell." (570)

After those words the bishop addressed the peasant again: "Let us now see your horse, which is wiser than the priest." They brought out the horse. (575) The peasant said before them all: "Lord, that horse is much wiser than the priest, as I will tell you. One morning I overslept. When I heard the sound of the bells (580) calling me to mass, I rushed quickly, since the church was far away.[6] I sat on my horse. I left the ordinary road at the side (585) and followed another path, which seemed to be much shorter so that I could arrive at mass in time. I rode through deep gullies and groves.[7] I followed a rough path with my horse. (590) At the end I reached a ditch over which I wanted to jump. My horse was so wise that it stepped forward carefully and fell down on its front feet (595). It returned, honestly, and refused to move forward. I spurred this wonderful horse hard to get going, but it fought me with all its might (600) and did not want to jump. But it suffered so much pain from me that it had to carry me down into the ditch, where we both ended up both falling down upon each other in the wide and deep bottom. (605)

With much suffering I managed to climb up, then I helped the horse to come out, and I reached the church in time before the Holy Eucharist had begun. I calmly stood in the church (610) until mass was over. Again I sat upon my horse and rode back on the same path. I looked for a good and solid road, but it did not get better. (615) Wherever I turned with the horse, I could not avoid the ditch and had to cross it again into which I had fallen before. I really thought (620) that it might work out better than before. But my horse was wise and not a fool. I spurred it forward with great force, much more than I had done before, (625) yet I could not make the horse do it. It was smart because it had fallen into the ditch. I had to give up my plan. So I turned to the road, (630) which was not so far, and rode there. Thus my horse had proven its intelligence.

The priest does not have such intelligence. I have to reprimand him for his misdeed, although I really do not like to do that, (635) but I cannot avoid it because if I do not defend myself I would be considered an evil person. The priest is the lover of the judge's wife. She loves him more than her own life, (640) for

---

[6] Literally: "wide over the fields."
[7] Literally: "deep moss, or swamp."

Schmalzturm (Grease Tower), Landsberg am Lech

which he has been beaten badly three times and severely wounded that he hardly recovered. Yet he does not want to let her go and sees her as previously. (645) Hence he is a fool and an idiot because he does not realize why he had to suffer so much pain before. He should leave her immediately, just as my horse (650) that no longer wanted to ride through the ditch in which it had suffered previously pain."

No. 4: *The Mayor and the Prince*

He who wants to acquire a good education and virtues should set as his goal to leave home and spend some time far away in foreign countries. (5) There he will have many adventures, both good and bad, as they might occur. He will thus acquire the skill (10) to keep guard from then on and forever protect himself from injuries. He will know this much better from his time abroad than from staying home, (15) as the proverb testifies: The child raised at home is called, and is indeed, a boor at court.

Now see, after lords send their children to universities who nevertheless have no interest (20) in turning into priests. They must gain a good education, virtue, and the experience necessary to achieve their goal. (25)[1] I have heard that the king of France sent his son, in good foresight, to the University of Erfurt. No one recognized him there (30) as the son of the king. I must honestly say: He lived quite luxurious lifestyle there. His heart was filled with great joy, buoyed by sweet love, (35) and women noticed him often. But his behavior was always virtuous.

One day it happened that evil thieves did their business. They had formed a gang (40) in that city; they stole many goods at night and thus caused much damage. They broke into the cellars and stores and opened them cleverly. (45) Both poor and rich people wondered who the thieves might be. They suffered dearly from them yet could not figure out who might be responsible for the losses. (50) Therefore the wise burghers of the city assembled in a council to consider how to cope with this danger quickly and find the culprits. One of them said: (55) "Listen to what I am thinking. Here in town there is a student who struts around everywhere in a luxurious manner together with many of his servants, but no one knows indeed (60) what his family background might be. He lives the high life at all time with the money available to him. Where does he draw all that money from that he is spending here in town? (65) It would be the lifestyle of a prince. I can only imagine that he must be associated with a company that secretly supports him. He causes us damage. (70) One ought to question who he is, since he

---

[1] This maxim became the standard principle for noble families in the late Middle Ages, who systematically sent their children to other courts or to universities to acquire the necessary education and worldliness; see Gerrit Deutschländer, *Dienen lernen*, 2012. Cf. also my review in *Sixteenth-Century Journal* XLIV.1 (2013): 307–8.

displays such courtly manners, and inquire who makes those means available to him. I am afraid that they might come from our treasure chests."

They all agreed with his words, (75) as I have to tell you honestly. The noble prince of France [orig.: king of France] attracted much suspicion from them all, as if he had committed the thefts. (80) But he was not accomplice of the thieves. They quickly agreed in unison that the mayor should go and see the noble and wealthy king (85) [the student]. The mayor, who was a very wise man, should talk with him diplomatically and carefully.

The mayor immediately went to see the noble prince, (90) who attended mass in a church. He said: "Honorable young man, the councilors of this city, that is, the members of the inner and the outer councils, have sent me to you. (95) In the name of your values and honor[2] please let me know what kind of life you lead and what your family background is. Allow me to ask these questions in friendly terms without begrudging me. (100) Whoever observes your manners and behavior, which are doubtless characterized by virtue and good education, recognizes without doubt (105) that you descend from a good family. Therefore please identify yourself. Once people know you, everyone will pay the respect and will offer you his service. (110) My fellow lords, who desire to be on friendly terms with you, want to find out about you, in good friendship and without any cunning."

The young king bowed his head (115) and looked at the burgher [mayor]. He thought to himself: "What kind of news is this?" and responded to the mayor: "This is rather astounding. Do you, in your council meetings, (120) have nothing else to do than to find out about me and from what family I originate? You are devoid of wisdom. Let me be who I am (125) and pursue other concerns that will be of more use for the city. I am not going to reveal the name of my family. God well knows who I am. I am not going to tell you more." (130)

The mayor [burgher] replied in polite words: "Lord, do not be angered by my words. By God's grace, as I say, you are most honorable. (135) My lords the councilors do not desire anything more than to enjoy your friendship. If you do not wish to divulge what family you belong to, then let me [at least] know the truth (140) from where your wealth derives, which you spend here richly together with your servants. You must certainly be a prince. If you let us know that, (145) then I can honestly tell you that people will pay you even more respect than before."

The king [prince] responded: "I am not going to tell you who I am. But you should not begrudge the goods and the profit (150) by which I live here and that I enjoy, even if I am a spendthrift. I live free of all cares because my income is very certain (155), as I collect it from every house here in the city every week, but

---

[2] These are key cultural terms prevalent especially since the late twelfth century, "zuht und . . . er," and they imply many different values, including education, manners, good behavior, idealism, honor, etc. See Otfrid Ehrismann, *Ehre und Mut*, 1995, 65–70, 248–53.

do not mind it and do not be cross with me. (160) All wives in every house pay me, without hesitation or fear, half a pound every week. Likewise, the house-maids pay me half that amount, (165) thus I have an infinite income. Should I not therefore live a fabulous life? After all, every week I make about a hundred pounds or more."

The mayor became deeply frightened. (170) He left right away. He was as hurt as if having received a wound from a sword. He met his companions and informed them what he had been told by the king [student]. (175) All their wisdom was destroyed thereby, all their glory gone, and they wished they had never inquired about him [the student].

Soon thereafter it happened that the mayor was sitting (180) at home to-gether with his beautiful wife, who was the delight of his heart. He suddenly spied the attractive young king [prince] walking across the market square. The burgher began to smile, (185) which his very sweet wife noticed. She asked: "My dear lord [husband], what is the reason for your smiling?" He said: "I will not tell you that." The wife was determined to find out (190) the cause of his behav-ior. She grabbed the man's chin with her snow-white hands and pulled it toward her lips. She said: "Explain why you are smiling! (195) My heart desires to know it." When he realized how serious she was, he said to his wife: "Do you see the young man down there standing next to the other students? (200) Every week he receives, from every household, to be sure, half a pound from each tender wife; nor are the housemaids exempt, since they give him half of that amount. (205) That way he plays the game of love."

"Horrors!" cried the lady immediately, "may he be cursed forever who makes such demands! Not even for a miserable penny (210) shall my house be indebted to him, neither from me nor from my maid" [i.e., she would never pay him for his love service]. However, she thought to herself, "Why has this guy been negligent of me (215) and not asked me for money in this good house?"

Inflamed by passion her heart began to burn. She paid close attention to the lord [the prince] (220) and cautiously made contact with him so that he became lovesick, because the rays of love had struck him. Both thus acquired a strong passion for each other, (225) which caused the mayor great pain. His wife dis-played such behavior that he could not help but fear the worst. He knew in his heart that he had talked too much (230) [about the student and his affairs].

One day the burgher had to travel and he entrusted the house to the care of his wife. He said: "In three days I will return." He then departed. Once the master of the house had left, (235) the pretty wife immediately thought, because of her heart's desire, how she could bring to her the student with whom she was infatuated. She had a smart housemaid, (240) who was loyal to her without fail. The wife revealed her secret desires to her and sent her to the student. The maid informed the latter what her mistress had in mind and asked him to see her im-mediately (245) in her private room, since the master of the house was not pres-ent. When the student heard that news, he rejoiced. He secretly went right away

(250) to his dearly beloved. Both of them felt great joy and delight without any limit, in fact, more so than I imagine I could reveal to anyone. (255) Neither one had ever experienced more joy in their lives. The lady did not hesitate and did not want to wait any longer, so she had a bath prepared (260) in a wide large tub. The student and the lady sat in the tub wearing no clothing and had no worries.

Now the above mentioned burgher [mayor] secretly returned to the house. (265) He clearly noted that something was not right. He did not commit any error, himself, however; he acted as a wise man who knows how to hide his shame from the public. (270) He went alone into the room where his wife was sitting [in the tub] with the student enjoying her time. Now, pay attention: [the mayor] greeted him [the student]. (275) The student and the woman became deeply frightened in this terrible situation; they felt that they had no option but to die. Then the lord of the house began to speak: (280) "My lady, do not be frightened, take good care of the guest. I will not hurt either of you." He took their clothes and locked it in a chest. (285) This way the host was safe from the guest, since the latter was naked. Thus, the student's joy came to an abrupt end. The lord said to the guest: "Fear not, (290) your life will not be harmed by me. Be nice to my wife!"

The lord stepped out of the room and quickly locked the door. This frightened the guest even more. (295) Now he felt great anxiety, because the burgher might attack him with his friends and relatives. However, the mayor spared the guest all pain. He brought him food and white wine, (300) as he intended to offer him a good meal after the bath, as good hosts tend to do. Both sat in front of him in the tub. They both were checkmated. They desired neither food nor drink (305) and could not think of anything they could do, and that resulted from their shame and fear. The host said to them both: "Your life and property will be safe from me, you can believe that on my honor." (310) He pledged this to them with his hand. He brought them their clothing again, and they both got dressed. Then the attractive guest and the wife had to sit down at table. (315) The husband brought venison and good fish and sat down next to them. He said to his wife: "Take good care of the guest, give him to eat and fill his glass. (320) Make sure that he does not get too little, since he deserves that in your name." The good student answered him: "Your worth and honor have not been impinged, since I have not done anything against you. (325) These strange events, in which you have observed me, have certainly happened without causing you any damage or for certain any loss." (330)[3]

When he finished speaking, the host said to him politely: "I want to ask you, my dear guest, that you will never again impose such a hardship on my house (335) because of money owed to you every week from my wife, that is, half a pound, and from the housemaid, that is, a quarter. I tell you that honestly. (340). He took from his pocket a handful of money and more, from which he paid out

---

[3] This is only true insofar as the couple has not yet slept with each other; otherwise the mayor's honor has already suffered a bad injury.

five shillings and half a pound for the maid and his wife. (345) He said: "Collect the money from me! This is the toll for this and following weeks. I will send you straight away the payment every week forever without any break, (350) but assure me then that you will never again come personally into my house, as you have done this time." (355)

The worthy guest replied: "Dear host and my lord, your house does not owe me this debt, neither from the lady nor the maid. I would feel truly sorry (360) if I ever entered your house again, unless upon your express wish. Now, previously you had asked me, which distressed me considerably, of what family I originate (365) and how I can live so carefree. I did not provide you with an answer then. I arrogantly told you that no one should worry about me because I drew my income and the large amount of money (370) from each individual house here. No one should be surprised that I can live here in such luxury because each housewife gives me [as I claimed] half a pound per week (375) and the house maids without fail give me five shillings per week. I actually spoke those words in jest, not meaning them to be true.

Now, let me tell you honestly (380) in good friendship and with repentance [for what I said before], what I did not want to do before, namely who I am and of what family I originate. I will also reveal where I get all my money from (385) that I have spent in the city. This should not surprise you, since I have gained my wealth, worth, and honor certainly through God's grace: I am the [future] king of France. (390) My father has sent me here to acquire good manners and virtues."[4]

When the host heard those words, he was very glad that he had not avenged himself against the prince. (395). He modestly stood and bowed before the high-born prince. He let go all his displeasure and wrath. Again the good king [prince] spoke: (400) "Good host and my friend, I will sponsor you forever in my country, because I know that you make your living (405) in my father's country with your merchandise. You have demonstrated many virtues toward me. Truly, you shall profit from it; (410) I will give you my letter, and my father will do so as well, confirming with his document that, when you enter my country, your body and your goods (415) will be well protected from any injuries. Wherever you will travel through forest or over open land, you won't have to pay anything for the protection by guards. Moreover, you will not have to pay any toll on your goods, I promise that on my grace." (420)

The host thanked him for that. Both were very happy about their agreement. Both their words and actions ended in friendship. (425) The mayor's wife remained unpunished by her husband because he was wise. He had dealt with the whole matter so quietly and silently that none of his servants or any other person knew anything about it. (430) The prince departed from him in friendship. He quickly sent to the wise man a good letter and also informed his father that he

---

[4] He really means to say: "education," but the traditional formula used here continues to imply only "good manners and virtues."

Alte Bergstraße (Old Mountain Street), Landsberg am Lech

had freed that man (435) in his whole country [from paying any toll], and his father should do so as well. He also told his father about the entire adventure from beginning to end. (440)

The burgher utilized the new conditions with all his ability and thus gained huge profit from his merchandise acquired in France. (445) From then on he grew considerably in honor and in great wealth. By his virtues and his wisdom he enjoyed happiness because he had not hurt the prince. (450) All this resulted in great wealth for him.

It is a gift of God to be graceful and to guard oneself from wrath; this is wise. A rash person ought to ride an ass (455) [because this is a slow moving animal] and ought to wait [in his actions] until his wrath has subsided. Thus he will never commit an error and protect his property; otherwise he might get into trouble. (460) After all, if the honorable burgher had caused great pain to the prince, he might easily have perished [himself]. Since he did not do so, he acquired great wealth, which he enjoyed right here. (465) May God grant us eternal life.

No. 5: *Payment for Love Service Returned*

He is a most blessed man who receives such honors from God that He grants him a virtuous wife, free from all cunning, who loves him with a loyal mind (5) and stands by him so closely that all of his property, his honor, and his goods, are well cared for and protected. I have thought about this and had an interesting adventure (10) that happened some time ago; I want to tell you about it now.

A young and spirited knight lived in a strong castle. He was honorable, virtuous, (15) well-built and of good looks, but he did not have much material wealth. Honestly, I have to say that his forefathers had spent it all [wasted it away]. But he enjoyed highest respect as an honorable man (20) and would have pursued chivalry with all his might, yet he was short of the necessary funds, which made him very sad. (25)

Not far away from him lived an old, virtuous, and generous knight who had often broken his lance and shield [had exercised in knightly jousts] according to knightly customs (30) during his young days. It grieved him greatly that the young and good knight, who excelled in his manly character, had to stay home miserably (35) suffering from poverty and misery. The old knight felt very sorry for him. Because he was generous and also rich, he treated the young knight, (40) as if he were his good friend, lifting his sorrows. He sent for him immediately and told him the following: "My dear friend and companion, (45) your misery grieves me; I dislike it that you have to stay home and cannot practice chivalry, as your forefathers did. But you are a young man (50), strong and instilled with a fresh mind; you have good manners and [inner] nobility, so you deserve knighthood. Please, whatever I can do to help you out in this situation, (55) just let me know."

The young knight was happy and answered him, speaking with a free mind: "I do not have enough money, (60) so I cannot pursue what my mind desires." The old man replied in a polite manner: "I want to change your misfortune and lend you enough money, (65) if you agree and think it proper. I will purchase for you two good horses,[1] a lance, and a shield, and whatever else you might need.

---

[1] Unclear, but the context implies that he means "horse." Normally the term "maid" means "young woman," or "virgin." Sappler, in his vol. II, 91, *Indices*, translates "maiden" as 'stallion.' For examples in Middle High German literature where "meide" means "horse," see http://woerterbuchnetz.de/cgi-bin/WBNetz/wbgui_py?sigle=Lexer&lemid=LM00891 (last accessed on Sept. 5, 2014); Konrad von Würzburg, in his *Partonopier und Meliur* (ca. 1280), uses this word (for "horse") quite commonly, such as in v. 620.

(70) You can repay me when you can, and you will not lose in honor if you take it all from me, because I recommend it to you myself. If God is graceful to you, (75) granting you good luck, then I will be repaid very well. If it turns out differently, and may God protect you from that, then you will be certainly free (80) from the obligation to pay me or my heir back."

The young man thanked him deeply. The old and worthy knight did not deliberate for very long (85) and bought him two great horses for sixty guilders or more, then also a mail-coat, a shield, and a lance, and whatever else a knight requires; he got it all, (90) so he was ready for knightly practice and serious battle. He also handed over to him, without being asked, for living expenses sixty gold ducats. He sent him a worthy servant, (95) who was loyal without fail. As the young man was now ready, the old knight told him that time a court festival had just been announced (100) in a very distant city. A large crowd of knights would arrive there from many different places, intent on displaying their accomplishments (105), and on impressing the sweet and beautiful ladies through demonstrations of their knightly skills of fencing and jousting. That was where the old man instructed the young knight to go.

The latter did not want to wait any longer (110) and said goodbye right away. He crossed mountains and flat land and aimed for the city. One evening it became very late and night fell, (115) as knight and his servant camped in a field. They found their rest under a tree. The knight said to his servant: "Stay here with my horses (120) and take good care of them while go for a walk in order to find some adventure in the forest."

He walked for about half a mile and came to a hedge of thorns next to a high fence. (125) He walked a long time parallel to it until he saw a light shining through the fence, which delighted him. He saw a splendid mansion (130) from where the light shone [on the ground]. Underneath a small doorway on the wonderful building the lord of the house was standing well protected (135). Truly, he held the light in his hand. His wife was walking down below him in a beautiful orchard. She looked miserable (140) and uttered loud laments about her teeth. The lord illuminated her from high up at the doorway so that she did not run into problems. He called to her: "My dear wife, (145) has your pain not subsided by now down at the fence? The beautiful woman replied: "My toothache increases here at the fence." (150)

The young knight heard all those words while he was standing there. He continued walking, following a narrow, crooked path, until he found a little door (155) which was open. He entered through the door and found the tender woman standing in the orchard, where she was waiting (160) for her beloved. She immediately realized that a knight had entered. She approached him, thinking that he was the one whom she expected, (165) and said without hesitation: "Is it you, my dear beloved?" He said: "Yes, my dear young lady!" But then he did not say another word; he was afraid that the lady would recognize (170) that he was not the right person. He lied her down in the grass and his heart's desire was fulfilled.

Then the lady realized (175) that he was not her lover, for whom she had waited for a long time. She was filled with pain and said: "Woe is me, poor woman! You have made love with me, (180) yet I do not know who you are. Tell me whether you are of a good family! A noble and sweet knight was supposed to sleep with me. (185) Woe and always woe! You received what he was supposed to enjoy."

The good knight responded: "Dear woman, take heart! I am also a good knight. (190) I looked for an adventure here and I have found it. Chivalry brought me here, and I intended to risk my life (195) in the service of all pure women." She said: "If that is true, my sorrow would be reduced. If you are such a man, then leave something behind for me (200) when you leave [at the end]; thus I will be able to confirm whether good education and nobility rest in you." He said: "Truly, at this point I have in my possession nothing but sixty gold guilders." (205) She replied right away: "Give me those! I will never forget you." He immediately turned the money over to her and said: "Lady, I urge you, (210) let me also have something with which I can remember you." The noble and beautiful woman gave him a reddish-gold ring. It was valuable, (215) but the exchange was unequal, because the ring was worth only eight gold guilders.

The knight went back, while the good husband still stood upstairs in the door and shone the light down into the garden, (220) listening to her words so that he could shorten her time [of alleged suffering]. He believed that she suffered great pain from her bad teeth. (225) She, however, longed for another man. The husband called down to her again: "Lady, do you feel better now?" She answered this fool right away (230): "My pain has lessened." Then she entered the castle again, and I will leave it with that.

The praiseworthy young knight returned to his servant (235) waiting underneath the tree, where he had left him with the horses. The lord told him what had happened. He also told him in detail (240) how he had given the sixty guilders to the beautiful woman, for which she had given him the ring of reddish gold. He showed it to the servant (245) which pleased the latter very much. He said: "My dear lord, be happy about it. Do not regret the guilders! God has accepted us as His servants (250) and secures our nourishment. Truly, I have to say that an adventure that involves the game of love is much better for a worthy knight (255) than all his goods and whatever he might possess."

After their exchange they took their rest and slept until the dawn of the next day. The servant woke up and jumped to his feet. (260) He took the horses and saddled them. Then he went to his lord and softly woke him up. The latter behaved as if he were sad, (265) which grieved the servant very much. He then said to his lord: "Lord, it seems to me as if you are unhappy. Why are you suffering; let me know!" The knight replied (270): "I am an unknown foreigner, how may I travel through this land without any money? This really worries me." The servant had good advice: (275) "God will take good care of us," he said to his lord. "I have enough money in my pocket for this day. Then God will arrange it (280) so that we can move forward. Do not despair!"

After their conversation they soon reached a large forest, which was four miles long and wide. (285) Now it was time to eat, and they spied a beautiful village beyond the forest. They rode to the inn-keeper, who welcomed them (290) and prepared them a meal. At that moment the lord of the village in which the innkeeper lived arrived. The lord was an old and good knight (295) who also intended to travel to the court, where the young knight wanted to seek knighthood. The old virtuous knight (300) also came into the inn. In truth, I tell you that it was the same knight who had stood in his castle (305) doorway, providing light to his wife who had a toothache and had looked for relief in the garden, until the splendid knight (310) slept with her without making noise, replacing her dearly beloved.

The two lords washed their hands [took water] and sat together at the table in proper fashion. (315) Neither knew the other. The old man asked the young one, saying: "Dear lord, please tell me, in the name of your good virtue, where do you intend to travel? (320) I would like to know that." The young knight, who was upright and loyal, told him honestly: "Lord, I am searching for knighthood and adventure, without fear; (325) that's why I am on my way. I intend to ride to the tournament [court] in the city, where many other knights and heroes will assemble."

The old man said: "My heart is filled with joy that you want to travel there, (330), because I would like to be your companion, to die with you or gain victory." This pleased the young man. (335) Indeed, I tell you, they both swore each other companionship: whatever misfortune might happen to one of them would concern both. Food, general charges [maybe: for the horses], wine, (340) and whatever they consumed the old knight paid as a confirmation [of their friendship].

The young knight and the old man departed from there, together with him the old man (345) and both happily traveled on. When they got to the city, the old gentleman asked the young one to ride next to him to his inn, (350) and so their friendship increased. The young knight cut a splendid appearance and his virtues shone through. (355) For that reason the old knight, who was respectable and rich liked him very much. He provided him with everything, chainmail and other equipment that he would need in the tournament (360) and for public enjoyment. He got the knight a good horse for jousting, on which he sat right away. The old knight then went (365) to the site of the tournament full of joy.

Many other knights were there. A skilled knight[2] challenged the young knight with his lance, but he unhorsed him easily, which pleased the old man, (370) especially since his companion had won the first joust himself on the open

---

[2] The text only says: "ain ritter cluog," which would be, literally translated: "a smart knight."

field. Thereafter he toppled four knights from their saddle in quick succession. (375) The old man praised the young, good knight, and both were very pleased. What else should I tell you? The young man rushed back and forth (380) through the tournament and unhorsed a countless number of knights, proving to be the best among them all, so that in the end no one dared to raise his lance against him. (385) The outstanding knight completed everything throughout the tournament. No one caused him a wound except for small scratches. Indeed, he proved to be (390) the best in the tournament. Many noble ladies were mightily pleased, to whom he was a great joy. He received the highest honor (395) and gained much respect and recognition from great lords and noble ladies. They came to his inn (400) to acknowledge him publicly. They all enjoyed dancing and jumping, playing on harps and violins, and singing, all in his honor. (405)

One evening when the court festival was over the young knight sat at table with his companions. They drank white wine (410) and had a good time. The pretty wife of the innkeeper and her husband told them of many different adventures. (415) The old knight also began to tell many jokes. The young, splendid knight was asked by the old one not to hold back; (420) he should also tell a story. He said: "In all my life I have never experienced any adventure like one that happened when I wanted to come here to this city. (425) One evening [on my journey] it got too late and I had to set up camp outside, underneath a tree, for the whole night. In the evening I got bored[3] and left my servant, (430) to whom I had entrusted the horses. I fell upon a great adventure when I came to a beautiful and strong castle, well fortified. Below the castle was an orchard, (435) where I heard the voice of a noble lady who suffered badly from toothaches.

At that moment her husband came out of the castle and shone a light from high above his wife, while standing in a doorway, (440) trying to make it easier for her. But she certainly did not suffer from tooth aches. Instead she was longing for her lover, whom she had directed to come there. (445) I [was the lucky one who] got that lady. When I entered the orchard and she noticed me, I approached her silently, (450) as if I were the right man. She said to me quietly: 'Dear beloved, have you finally arrived?' I said right away: 'Yes.' Then I made love with her without delay (455). Subsequently she realized that I was not the right person. She spoke to me angrily: 'Who are you? You have miserably deceived me! (460) I thought you were my lover; he is a noble and fine knight, for whom I have waited for a long time here.' She did not want to believe that I also was of noble birth, (465) until I gave the fine lady sixty guilders. Thereupon she pulled off her finger a reddish-gold ring, which she gave me in return. (470) I left there filled with joy. But still the good old man shone the light for his lady so that she could get some relief [from her toothaches]."

---

[3] Literally: "the night seemed too long for me."

Once he had finished with this account, (475) the old man felt great pain in his heart and said: "Let us see the ring so that we can trust your report." The young man did not hesitate (480) and showed him the ring. The old man recognized immediately that it was his wife's ring. Secretly his suffering increased.

In the morning, at dawn (485) everyone got up. The mayor of the city and with him the entire council arrived and observed (490) that people were preparing their departure. Truly, I tell you the young, virtuous, and noble knight was honored by them and by his companions. (495) The city generously paid for them all the food, hay [for the horses], the rooms, and wine. They did so in his honor because he had garnered so much praise. His companion, the old knight (500) also benefited from that. They did not tarry longer, and prepared for their journey, and happily returned home.

When they reached a point (505) where they could see the castle that belonged to the old knight, he said politely to his worthy fellow: "See, my lord, that is my castle. (510) Tonight you must be my guest. I wish to house you well, and ask that you accept this invitation to stay the night with me." The young knight granted him that wish immediately. (515) A servant was sent ahead of them whom the old lord had charged as follows: "Tell my dear wife to prepare the house well. I am arriving and bringing with me (520) a wonderful noble knight. She should put on her best clothes and welcome him worthily because he wears the crown of honor."

The servant did not linger (525) and carried out the order of his lord. The lady also complied with his wishes and did everything the servant relayed to her well and properly. To tell the truth, (530) [however,] the young knight, though strong and worthy, was rather distressed. When he looked at the castle he said to his own servant: "It seems to me, honestly, (535) that this is the same castle, where I had that adventure not long ago. Up there is the little doorway where the lord (540) shone the light for his wife. Below is the orchard, the high fence and the hedge, along which I walked until I found the entrance. (545) I recognize this house. But I told the old man openly the entire adventure. Advise me, what shall I do? I am afraid great trouble (550) may come from our host."

"If he is an honest man," said the servant in reply, "he will neither cause us harm nor shame while we stay in his castle. (555) When we are leaving, and he might try to hurt us, then he will have to suffer from both of us."

They had reached the [draw]bridge in the meantime. The lady [of the house] had heard of it (560) and came out to meet them. She happily greeted the guest in a courtly manner, as did her husband. She took the guest by his hand (565) and took him into the house where he found an elegant and delightful room prepared for him, for which he expressed his gratitude. A great dinner was served. The host and his beautiful wife (570) showed great respect toward the guest. Cheerfully they ordered that wine, food, and other items be served.

When it became late and time to go to bed, (575) the good guest had to promise on his honor that he would not depart right away the next morning, because the host (580) wanted to get up early and go hunting. He also told him to wait until lunch because he wanted to deliver venison to the kitchen. (585) Because the guest was obliged to stay throughout the whole morning, he spent the entire night restlessly [filled with worries].

Before dawn the host went hunting in the forest with his huntsmen. (590) They soon caught a large deer; they had great fun capturing it. When the day broke, (595) the guest no longer wanted to sleep. He stood up and said his prayer. When he was finished, the lady arrived carrying out her duties [as a host], saying: "I hope you will not be bored (600) until the host has returned." The good knight responded: "I will do whatever you command." The lady said: "Then let us have some fun with a board game." (605) They did not hesitate for long, sat down together and played their game.

During that time the knight put the ring on his finger. (610) When the lady noticed that, she became very frightened and began to cry as a result of her heart-pain. She said: "My dear lord, (615) tell me from where you got that ring?" He said: "You know this just as well. You yourself gave it to me in return for sixty 60 gold guilders." The lady replied: (620) "My dear lord, you are so upright and loyal, has my husband ever seen it in your possession? Tell me that!"

He answered her in a friendly manner: "Unfortunately, he has seen it repeatedly. (625) This occurred often because I did not know either one of you." The lady replied immediately: "Oh dear me, what horrors! So I will have to suffer my death." (630)

When both had fallen victim of worry, the hunters returned with the huge deer. They were let into the castle. The lord also arrived back with them. (635) The guest and the noble lady were deeply worried. They no longer dared to spend time privately together. Then the joyful host (640) quickly entered the room of the worthy guest. He said: "I hope you have not been bored in my house during my absence." He ordered food and wine. The venison was soon prepared. (645) The joyful [young] knight sat down at table. The host and the sweet lady sat down with him at the table. Both venison and good fish (650) were served right away. What else shall I tell you? The guest was treated very well, the cups were constantly refilled from which they drank wine. (655)

When the cook entered the room and the tables were cleared, the lady sat there filled with worries. Since the guest now wanted to depart, she was afraid that her husband (660) might punish her. The guest clearly noticed that in her, which concerned him deeply. The noble and worthy host said to the lady: (665) "Now, upon your honor, have you known the guest from before?" She immediately responded: "Why do you ask me that, my dear lord? Now, I am telling you honestly (670) that I have not known until now where he is from and who he is." The host responded: "How dare you say that you have no knowledge of him? (675) Where are the sixty guilders that he gave you? Go and bring those right away!" The lady became frightened by his words. She said: "I cannot bring (680) what I do not [even] have. I have not seen this guest before in my whole life except now." (685) He answered: "Where is the ring that I had given you when we married?" He did not let her go scot-free; he forced her upon threats to her life to return (690) the sixty guilders which she brought to both men, filled with sorrow. The host took them and put them on the table. (695)

Then he addressed both: "This is the law of all games in which the throwing of dice is involved. He who brings out the game board (700) ought to have his share. He who provides light should also have his share." He divided the sixty guilders equally into three parts. (705) In each pile there were twenty guilders, not more. One part he offered the guest and said: "Now, take the profit from the dice (710) that you have thrown on the board." The other pile he offered to the lady. He said to her: "Lady, take note, accept the red gold! (715) That is your pay-back for good game board, which you lent to him and on which he had his fun. The third pile belongs to me (720) for the light that I shone and with which I illuminated the scene."

Once the division had occurred, the guest politely spoke: "Dear lord, be in good spirits! (725) Let it all go now and spare me your wrath. The lady has lost your grace. But I will not depart from here until you will have granted to the lady (730) your grace again despite her lack of manners and her guilt. I beg you, lord, for that favor in the name of the companionship that we enjoyed together. (735)

The host said: "In the name of God! You have appealed to me most seriously. I cannot ever forget what we shared." He pledged truly to him (740) that he would not hurt his wife in any way in the future. The guest reestablished friendship and peace between the couple. (745) This made the lady deeply happy in her heart. The guest promised to the host that he would from then on and forever after be a good companion with all his strength (750) and provide him with service, to die with him or survive [in battle]. The virtuous and attractive guest departed from them in good friendship. He went home to his country, (755) which made his friends happy. He was recognized far and wide and soon gained both in honor and worldly goods, as happens to many knights (760) who know how to exert all their abilities. He also paid back the good man who had extended his friendship to him and who had first equipped him. Loyally he repaid him. (765) Thus this story has come to an end.

No. 6: *The Cowardly Husband*

A small injury is truly preferable to a permanent large one. Choosing between two bad things I would make that selection, as I would advise. If you have to decide for one thing, (5) let go the one that is a greater evil and accept the one that is a lesser evil. Better a person lose hands and feet [as a punishment] than to be interred [as the result of the death penalty]. If a city might burn down, better a person should decide (10) to tear down his own house so that a fire no longer spreads if he can prevent it from consuming the entire city. (15) Every thief who must give up his life and is handed over to the gallows gives proof of that understanding, requesting that in the name of honor they decapitate him instead. (20).

An adventure once happened, as one can read here, that applies to this saying to some extent, and yet not quite. I will present it to you now (25) and thus make it known. In Straßburg a rich man was married to a woman who was the most beautiful woman who had ever joined a man in marriage. (30) She displayed strong chastity, good manners, and many good virtues. Truly, I tell you, no one ever heard a thing about her (35) by which her honor would have been tarnished. All over the country people said the same thing, that you could not find among all women [among all red mouths = lips = women] (40) anywhere the world over a woman who was as respected, beautiful, and chaste as she, and who had as many good manners and great virtue as that one in the city of Straßburg.

An excellent knight, who roamed over all the countries, heard those rumors. (45) He had risked his worthy life many times on behalf of beautiful women, whom he served from early in the morning until evening. He traveled to that city (50) and stayed there for about half a year. Whenever he spied the lady he made himself known to her.[1] He addressed her without fear and in a friendly manner

---

[1] Here we encounter a good example to illustrate where I differ from Simmons's translation. The original clearly says: "wau er der frawen wart gewar," which is not the same as "When he became aware of the woman." After all, the knight had been on the look-out for her and pursued her diligently for the whole time. Admittedly, "gewar" seems to imply "aware," and is actually etymologically a cognate with Old High German "gawar," "giwar," and Middle High German "gewar" (see the entry for 'aware' in the OED [Oxford English Dictionary online at http://www.oxforddictionaries.com/us/definition/american_english/aware, last accessed on Sept. 5, 2014]), but the narrative context forces us to read it slightly but critically differently.

(55), which he knew how to do well, making many jokes.[2] This bothered the
chaste woman because she clearly recognized that what he wanted from her en-
dangered her honor (60). What he desired was painful to her heart, but he wooed
her so constantly that she could no longer stand it. (65) She was afraid that her
honor would be diminished through people's evil gossiping. She informed her
husband and complained about the great harassment that she suffered from the
foreigner. (70) He said: "My dear wife, I want to help you solve the problem.
When he speaks with you again, tell him to come and see you in your private
chamber. (75) Then I will hide in your room as well. I will pay him back for his
love wooing so much that from then on he will have to leave you completely in
peace." (80)

Three days later, when the knight went to church for mass according to his
usual pattern, the woman went up to him without any evil intentions. (85) He
immediately greeted her with loving and flattering words. He said: "May God
reward you! Dear lady, let me know now (90) how I can come to you, because
I suffer great [love] pains and more because of you. Let me tell you: no one can
help me to quench my pain (95) except you; no one else in the entire world." The
chaste woman replied: "You ought to come and see me after dinner in my house.
I intend to be at home by myself. (100) I will arrange it so that no one will dis-
turb us."

The knight had much joy from her words. He immediately left her, filled
with great joy. (105) Honestly, I must say, his heart was inflamed. Love's arrow
had shot into it at that moment, causing him a bad wound. (110) The slow passage of time while the priest sang the mass seemed excruciating to him.

When the right time arrived, he went to her house straight away and knocked
at the door. (115) The worthy lady went to the door and silently let him in. She
led him to her chamber and placed him on a beautiful couch. (120) They both sat
down on it. The husband had actually hidden behind a large barrel placed in the
room, as the lady knew well. (125) He had put on a strong armor and was ready
to cause the knight great sorrow. Now, the knight had arrived dressed only in a
tunic, (130) which was well made out of red gold. He looked as if he was ready
to dance with ladies, wearing no outer armor. On his side (135) he wore a strong
and elegant dagger. The pretty lady said to him: "It is a great foolishness of you,
my dear sir, that you have come here (140) without armor or a sword. You might
be [attacked and] hurt by my friends and relatives. I see that you wear a valuable
and elegant tunic, (145) as if you planned to go to a dance. True, you also wear a
knife, but it would not help you much, if someone tried to hurt you."

---

[2] Again, the vagueness of Kaufringer's words can lead to different interpretations.
Simmons understands "in rehtem schimpf" "as urbane manner" (38), but then renders the
following line, "als er wol kund mit gelimpf" thusly: "as he well knew how to, with many
deceitful words." "gelimpf," however, does not carry such a negative connotation. Sappler,
vol. II, *Indices*, 56, only lists the words but does not translate them.

The lady spoke those words (150) in a loud voice so that her husband would gain more confidence. But the valiant knight replied: "Lady, I am such a man that I am not afraid of anyone. (155) I tell you, I am so strong and have also such extraordinary courage that no one would be my equal, I swear by the truth of that. (160) Here I have a good knife from which no armor is safe."[3] An armored plate was hanging on the wall, which the knight quickly removed and placed it (165) openly in front of the woman. It was thick and consisted of six layers. He said to the woman: "Lady, now watch how strong I am!" He pulled out his knife (170), and with one stab he pushed it all the way through all six layers of the plate of armor. Then he spoke: "My knife is very good."

The husband stayed quietly in his hiding place. He became very frightened with those words. (175) He no longer dared to come out from behind the barrel, as he had originally planned. He thought to himself: "I must suffer the pain of misery, (180) if he notices me here." He was very afraid of the knight's strength. "No one can spare me from that excellent knife," (185) was his inner thought. "The armor will help me little, because he could stab through the strong plate in one try. I will remain here in my hiding place; (190) otherwise I might experience pain from him, whatever might happen to my wife."

The knight sat down again and moved close to the woman. He embraced her tenderly. (195) She said loudly: "What does that mean? I do not grant you any love. My husband is here in the house. If he realizes what is happening here, he will avenge himself." (200) What shall I tell you? The knight took the woman and carried her to the bed against her wishes, disregarding her pleading. She screamed loudly and for a long time, (205) but the knight overpowered her.[4] No one came to her rescue, which made her very angry. He who was supposed to provide her with help neglected her in her heartfelt suffering. (210) The knight forced himself upon her with his strength and wrestled her down, having his way with her.[5] That had not been the original plan of the wife and her husband, (215) who had expected a very different outcome.

---

[3] Simmons translates "messer" as "dagger," which might fit better overall, but I prefer the literal rendering as "knife" because it underscores the small size of the knight's weapon in contrast to the husband's sword. Of course, "dagger" ultimately also would work.

[4] For future discussions of this passage, the narrator leaves no doubt as to the fact that the woman is raped, although at first sight it might appear to be more like date-rape. The situation is difficult; she had invited him in to her private chamber, she had promised him her love, but now she explicitly rejects him, screams for help, and is physically, i.e., sexually, abused, whereas the knight does not understand at all her changed attitude and disregards all her protests.

[5] I have adapted several words used by Simmons without quoting them since she offers a stylistically better version than what I had in mind at first.

Once the wife had been raped by the knight, she cried from the bottom of her heart because she had been hurt deeply in her honor, (220) shamefully and yet without the knight having pursued an evil desire. The knight tried to console her with sweet words, which almost caused her death, because she could not feel friendly toward him. (225) She did not offer him either peace or reconciliation; instead she reproached him bitterly, so he departed from her, filled with sadness in his heart. He really did not understand (230) what he had done there, neither good nor bad.

When the woman realized that the noble knight had left the house (235), she quickly went to the barrel and found the "brave hero," who held a sword in his hand, with armor reaching up to his neck. She addressed him with bitter words (240): "Why are you resting here, you evil dog? How dare you abandon me in this great suffering! I almost died; if only I would have been saved. (245) What were you thinking about when you chose not to help me?" He answered, trying to appeal to her [with friendly words]: "Be quiet, my dear wife, and let what happened be. (250) Believe me, I will never think badly about you and your honor and do not say (255) that I have been neglectful. I did not take any action for the following reasons: a small injury is certainly better than a great one, be assured of that! (260) If I had done something against him, he would not have spared me with his strength that he possesses. He would have stabbed me right away through my armor, (265) which is not as strong as that plate of armor [through which he had stabbed his knife]. So I would then have died. That would have been a great injury indeed. (270) Certainly, you have suffered pain, but it is called and really is only a small injury from which you can recover."

In fact, I have to say that he was right and yet not quite, (275) because if he had quickly intervened before the woman experienced suffering [rape] and had not attacked the knight physically, then the rape would not have happened (280)[6] and his dear wife would not have experienced a "little" injury nor would he himself have been hurt either. But since he had made up his mind to stay hidden, (285) it is just that he suffer shame and blame. He is an evil guardsman who observes and sees another man hurts [rapes] his good friend [wife] (290) without rushing to his [her] help. I wish upon him misery until his death. May God grant that he will not achieve anything he might desire! (295) There is nothing worse that I could wish for him.

---

[6] The original is ambivalent: "ungemach" means "little damage" or "little injury." But the English word is too weak in this context, so contrary to Simmons I resort to the much stronger term "rape," which clearly specifies what the knight did to the woman.

No. 7: *The Monk as Love Messenger, B*

A person who wants to enter a love affair and search for one must be very inventive. He must plan well about how to proceed in this matter so that he will have the success (5) he desires. Now, I do not know anyone currently who could come up with such good plans and arrange a love affair as clever women do. They achieve the goals (10) they desire with intelligence plans. What no one ever imagined before they manage to achieve. While having just made these comments, (15) I remember an adventure that I want to tell you confirming my remarks. My words illustrate my observations, so let me begin with my story.

In Augsburg lived a valiant young man who daily walked around, (20) both in the morning and the evening, many times each in order to catch sight of his beloved on the street where she lived. He acted like every good lover. (25) He was attractive and in good spirits. Now, a ['loose'] woman lived nearby who was very open-minded who liked the young man very much. To tell the truth, (30) she longed for him, and was wounded by the love arrow that had hit her heart. She suffered from her love for the young man, both early in the morning and in the evening (35). She ruminated about how quietly to inform the young man decently, without anyone else learning about it.

There was a pious monk, old and ailing, (40) who was a divine person. He had reached the age of eighty years. The lady and the monk were good companions (45) with each other; it was all proper between them. She went to the good monk as if she were bothered by something and said: "I beg you, lord, in the name of God, to free me from suffering and mockery (50) which I experience every day. Now, listen to my complaint because I do not trust anyone as well, as you, my very beloved lord." (55) He said: "I'll alleviate your sorrow as much as it is in my power." She answered: "Honestly, I tell you, a young man here in town daily walks up and down in front of my house, (60) richly dressed. Lord, it troubles me because he wants to be my lover, which impinges on my honor. This is not proper (65) because, if my husband notices it, or some of my maids, I will have much unrest. I beg you, dear lord, let the young man know (70) that he ought to leave me in peace and respect my honor."

The monk said to her: "I know the young man well (75).[1] I will impose a penance on him, as is my duty. He has always been obedient to me. I will

---

[1] We have no idea how the monk would have recognized that man without further identification markers, but that is beside the point of this story.

convince him not to cause you any evil." Three days later (80) the monk spoke to the young man when he found him in church: "Now listen to me, my dear son, immediately stop with your business in the street (85) where the lady lives. She complained heavily to me that you walk up and down there every day, which creates much gossip. If her friends will see that (90), they would punish her for that." The young man said: My dear lord, I have no affair with her, either in appearance or out of lustful desire, believe me upon my honor! (95) She will not be bothered by me in any possible way, by whatever might hurt her reputation. I also have never harbored any ill plans against her, neither in words nor in deed." (100)

That was good enough for the monk. Truly, I must say, both were completely ignorant and did not know the secret plans the woman pursued. (105) None of them comprehended her intentions. The young man then said goodbye and left. He returned, as before, looking[2] for his own beloved, walking up and down the street, (110) as a lover is expected to do. The woman, who had visited the monk, noticed that well and gazed out of the window even more, showing her delightful face. (115) The young man did not pay attention to her and completely ignored her, because he had not come there for her. This grieved the woman greatly. Her pain grew and increased (120) more than ever before. Again she returned to the old monk and said: "Lord, your efforts and your penalty have unfortunately not helped. (125) [The young man] now appears even more than ever before. People have begun to notice it and talk much about it. I am afraid of bad consequences (130) and am afraid for my life; perhaps my husband might notice what is going on." The monk replied, angrily: "But he had sworn to me and pledged by his honor (135) that he was quite innocent in that matter in both words and in deeds. He also said that he does not desire you as his mistress. But I will reprimand [punish] him even more; (140) he must leave you alone, or lose my grace."

The next day the monk encountered the young man standing near the monastery. (145) He approached him and spoke angrily: "You are neither virtuous nor good, because you have broken what you had clearly promised me on your honor. (150) Your [behavior] endangers the lady's life with your great arrogance. Everyone on the street and all the neighbors are talking about you, (155) which means that the virtuous and chaste woman has almost lost her honor. You must follow my advice, leave the woman in peace. She does not want you as her lover." (160)

The young man politely replied: "Honestly, lord, your wrath and anger grieve me. I had sworn to you before that I am completely innocent regarding that woman, (165) both in words, intentions, and deeds. More I cannot say. I walk up and down the street without thinking about her; I do not impinge thereby on her honor. (170) I care as little as you do about her, believe me that."

---

[2] I have expanded the expression slightly to give the full sense of what the man is doing, while the original only states: "gieng wider zuo dem puolen sein" ("went back to his beloved").

Let us pause here. The young man did not want to stop his former behavior and returned looking for his beloved, (175) walking up and down the street many times, both day and night, and playing the game of love. Nevertheless, he noticed that the other lady openly and often (180) looked at him from the window. I mean the one lady who had complained about him to the monk. She friendly cast her gaze at him. The young man thought by himself that she might be doing that with evil intent. (185) He then left and did not want to look back at her. He wanted to stay true to what he had promised the monk. He [deliberately] acted meanly (190) and turned his head [neck] away from her. That caused the noble lady such deadly pain that she began to shed bitter tears. She thought: "How do I achieve (195) my intentions better than I have done thus far? I must figure out another strategy. The words of the monk do not have their effect. I will pursue another approach (200) in order to show my dear beloved the true intent of my heart."

The lady immediately ordered a ring to be made for her (205) with letters engraved clearly and finely written. They said the following: "Pay attention and try to understand this!" When the ring was ready, she pretty lady went straight away (210) to the place where she found the monk. She cried much and told him straight away: "Lord, I want to let you know what that evil man has done to me, he who had promised you before (215) not to do anything evil against me ever. He has transgressed badly against me, dear lord. There is a thorny fence not far (220) behind my garden. At night he came there when it had turned dark. He climbed over it, then stepped over the outer wall (225) and jumped down and walked toward my garden. There he considered how he could enter.

He discovered a tree growing close to the wall, (230) which he climbed up. When he had found his way into the garden he went to the house. He found the door open; the maid had forgotten (235) to lock it. Thus he entered the house. The door to my room was open. Quietly he came in. In his foolish manner (240) he lay down on the bed next to me. I said in a loud voice: "Who are you?" He asked me to be quiet, but I did not. I screamed in a loud and great voice, (245) making the entire house echo. I jumped up angrily. With difficulty I freed myself from him, and if the maid had not arrived, he would have caused me great sorrow (250). She helped me out of my great danger. He then ran out of the house because he wanted to keep it all a secret.[3] Lord, see this ring. (255). That is clearly proof. He really wanted to give it to me. I did not want to accept it, but he placed it on a window sill for me."

---

[3] The Middle High German uses the conditional case, but the meaning is simply causal without the use of the subjunctive.

Then she showed it to the monk. (260)[4] He took it into his hand and said: "Dear young lady, I deeply grieve in my heart, he assured me so much before to the contrary and denied everything. (265) I will never believe him again, and will not refrain from imposing a penalty on him." The woman encouraged him strongly: "Lord, ask him to come to you soon, (270) if not right away. I cannot tolerate much more waiting. He might otherwise cause me sorrow. That fool could be rather dangerous for me." Having spoken, (275) the lady left the cleric.

The monk called the young man to him, who arrived quickly. Full of wrath the monk spoke to him: "You cause me great discomfort (280) and so also this poor woman. Indeed, you are a real rogue. Whatever promises you make to me, you yourself break." Word by word he repeated the story (285) and told him in detail, everything the woman had informed him about: what he had done at night, how he had climbed over the high fence, and from there quietly and watchfully (290) onto the tall circular wall, and how he then had gone to the tree growing aside the house, climbing it skillfully, and from which he then had jumped down into the garden; (295) how he had found the house door open, how he got into the chamber and had embraced the woman,[5] whom he had intended to shame [rape]. But the good maid (300) had rushed to her lady's help. All that he told him and much more: "The lady does no longer want to be pestered by you, (305) otherwise she will, as I tell you on my honor, complain to her friends. At this point she will not do so, as I strongly asked her for that intensively. I tell you that honestly." (310)

The young man managed to say the following: "I will not cause her any harm, on my honor, I am not guilty of what you have told me." (315) But the monk did not let it go with that. He gave him the ring and said: "That was yours; you left it in the house. She does not want it. (320) She is returning it to you through me. The words on it confirm that all the woman says is true, whereas your words mean nothing, (325) as I recognize and perceive them in my heart."

Now, the young man took the ring into his hands and looked at it carefully. He found carved into it: (330) "Pay attention and try to understand this!" As he read that, he secretly thought: "That woman has appealed to me often, yet I never understood it right." (335) Turning to the monk he said: "I promise you firmly, I will handle the matter now in such a way that the woman will henceforth not complain about me. (340) Believe that for sure." That was enough of an assurance for the monk. The young man then left.

When evening arrived, (345) he walked to the house and noticed the garden and the thorny hedge next to it. He clearly saw (350) how to get into the garden

---

[4] Here is a typical line filler with the adverbial expression: "vil pald," which does not mean anything in this context, except "very quickly," which is unnecessary for the translation of this passage.

[5] The text is not quite clear here and does not make full sense; literally: "and how he took the woman" — hence better: "embraced her."

at night to reach his clever mistress. When it was night, he went there quietly. When he found the hedge of thorns, (355) he climbed over it. Then he reached the circular wall. He observed that the tree next to the house offered the desired opportunity; he climbed down on it (360) and so reached the garden without falling and without difficulty. He saw that the house door was open, so he entered it right away. (365) He reached her room, which was not locked and was open for him. There he found the worthy lady resting in the bed. Very quietly he lay down next to her (370) as if he were her beloved darling. This is true and not contrived. He was a very welcome guest and not a threat to her, as the pious and good monk had believed (375) in his simple mind. The woman immediately recognized that he was the man she loved and for whom her heart was filled with longing. The pretty and clever woman (380) enjoyed her time with him. Both their hearts were filled with delight. She fulfilled everything his heart desired from her.

What else can I say? (385) The splendid young man spent a wonderful night with the woman, without threats or reprimands as she had made before (390) when she had talked to the monk. She never returned to complain about the young man.

With these words I praise women who are so wise and filled with clever ideas. (395) They know how to arrange it so that they realize their plans by teaching a monk through clever and subtle lessons, thus making him the messenger (400) through whom they accomplish their love affairs.[6] Was not the monk rightfully punished by the abbot, his master, although he suffered his penalty unjustly because he was so ignorant[7]? (405) Thus my story comes to an end.

---

[6] The narrator switches from plural to singular here.

[7] This implies that the actual story continued with the love affair having been revealed, with the monk having been identified as the culprit, hence his punishment. But the narrator ignored all that.

No. 8: *The Search for the Happily Married Couple*

I have often heard an old proverb that a man and his wife should have two souls and one body together. (5) What happens to the one, whether it be good or bad, happens to both of them. They are supposed to be in such a union that if one of them wants something full-heartedly (10) and really takes pleasure in it, then the other should agree to it as well. This might then be called a pure life and can truly be counted as a perfect marriage. (15)

I would like to tell you a true story. Once there was a rich burgher who enjoyed great respect and honor. He was generous and high-spirited and descended from a good family (20). He was respectable and virtuous and enjoyed much honor. He lived a grand life. His heart was filled with great joy when his good friends (25) visited him at home. He liked to have them with him because he did not like to miss their company. He was married to a virtuous woman whom he loved as much as his own life. (30) She commanded much honor and respect, and was blessed with countless virtues. She happily fulfilled his wishes, but the husband suffered much sorrow from his good wife (35) because he was so generous and enjoyed company at home. She was angry with him because she was rather miserly. When her husband would tell her (40) that he wanted to host company, she chastised him. This greatly pained the husband. If he pulled toward one direction, she pulled toward the other. She was too miserly, he was too generous. (45) I do not reprimand the wife, however, because she was submissive to him in all other respects.

One day her husband was sitting by himself and ruminated as follows: (50) "How is it possible that everywhere in the city my wife is praised by all for having infinite virtues, (55) honor, and respectability. They even say that she is free of all instability. To me this seems a foolish idea because she causes me sorrow and suffering (60) with her evil miserliness. The entire city assumes, and says so as well, that she follows my wishes entirely. In reality she is totally opposed to me, indeed, more than anyone knows, (65) I have suffered from it secretly for a long time, and I cannot tolerate it any longer. We are not of one body as everyone says and thinks about us. (70) In fact, I will search anywhere in the entire world to find two virtuous and pure married people who are so much of one mind that each agrees with the other (75) whatever she or he might think, without them having a fight and struggle. I am determined to carry out this plan. (80)"

The man immediately prepared himself for a long journey and took much travel food with him, since he had unmeasurable wealth. Officially he said that he wanted to do business as a merchant, (85) trusting his good fortune. Then this virtuous and respectable man rode off with a servant to see many major cities. (90)

Whenever he reached a bigger city he did not mind spending considerable time trying to find searching, (95) as far as this was possible, two married people united fully in mind and attitude who did not suffer from conflicts, fights, or bickering. He traveled so long (100) that he consumed a great amount of his money, and yet he did not discover anywhere such good and pure married people [as he was looking for]. (105) Nevertheless, he chose not to return home, until he used up all his money first.

Thus he spent four years. In the fifth year he arrived at a magnificent city (110) that was great and wealthy. Here as well he intended to spend some of his travel money. He lived for about half a year with a rich burgher (115) who was loyal and very trustworthy. He was married to a virtuous wife. In words, actions, and in their minds they handled everything the same. No one observed any fighting or conflict between them. (120) I must tell you truly, the worthy traveler was very pleased about this. He said to his servant: "Indeed, I have found here (125) what I have been looking for numerous years. Now we can ride home."

When the host realized that the guest wanted to depart, he said very politely (130) and in private to his host: "I beg you, my dear sir, and consider it only as a friendly gesture, that you let me know what your business has been here. (135) You cannot find much commerce here that might be fruitful for your country. Therefore my mind tells me that you are looking for adventure here. My heart would really be pleased (140) if I could learn right now what it might be, and this request comes in full friendship and without any evil intent." Immediately the guest answered him: "In secret I will let you know what my intentions are. (145) Back home I am married to a proper, virtuous, and good wife. All my possessions are well protected and cared for by her. She complies with all my wishes, (150) but in one aspect she fails. I am very unhappy about one blemish in her—she is a little too miserly. She always chastises me for trying hard to gain public recognition [by being generous and hospitable]. (155) In this matter she is very different from me. I left home because I thought to myself that I would never return until I had found two virtuous married people (160) who fully shared the same ideas. These I have now discovered in the fifth year best represented by you and your wife. (165) Therefore I shall not stay any longer and will prepare to go home." Thereupon the host said right away: "You ought to stay here one more day with me, (170) then I will show you what the common life between my wife and myself is really like." The guest replied: "I will happily stay, my dear sir." (175)

The host invited his friends and enjoyed great festivities with them. No one was bored. Many musicians performed, and the group was accompanied by many beautiful ladies. (180) One could hear beautiful songs, and later the women danced gracefully. The host's wife was joyful, and her heart leaped for happiness. The guest was very pleased with it. (185) Truly, I tell you, they celebrated all day until late at night. Once the party concluded and everyone had gone home, the host spoke (190) with his esteemed guest.

He said: "You have seen my wife act today as if she were in a good mood, and that was the case. (195) But now I want to let you know the true reason for it, which is also why I held you back and why I celebrated this festival with my wife. Often pain follows happiness, (200) and after joy follow heartfelt laments. Similarly my wife has spent the present day full of joy, of which she could gain much. But now you will observe (205) and understand most thoroughly that this joy cannot last forever. Afterward painful complaints always ensue for my wife, as she has brought it upon herself."

Thereupon he quickly addressed the woman[/wife]: (210) "Now bring your drinking vessel. Then I will pour your St. John's love drink [a memorial or good-bye drink] which I have right here. Afterward we can go to sleep."

The woman became very frightened upon hearing his words. (215) "I will never bring the drinking vessel out here," she said, "you can believe that! I would rather suffer the pain of death. What are your intentions with me today? Allow me to drink it (220) in your presence only in the bedroom, my dear husband, as I am used to doing".

The husband did not grant her this wish: instead he went and brought the drinking vessel himself and placed it in front of the timid woman, (225) which hurt her greatly. She was deeply ashamed in front of the guest, whose presence intensified her embarrassment. The vessel was a human skull, into which the host poured (230) the white wine without hesitation. Then he said to her: "See, now take and drink what I brought you: the love of St. John." The wife did not fight against it because she did not dare to oppose her husband. (235) She drank from the cup sorrowfully.

The host then spoke to the guest: "Sir, this is the misfortune that I witness every night. Whenever I want to go to sleep, (240) my wife, who has no other choice, has to drink from this human skull, which I tore out of the head of a priest. I found him lying with my wife while he made love with her. (245) I killed him and secretly buried him so that no one knows his whereabouts. I took his skull as a pawn, (250) and my wife has to drink from it. For five years now she has had to go through this penance every night. I have decided that I will never absolve her from it; (255) she will have to perform this penance for the rest of her life, and no one will be able to change that."

When the guest had heard these words, he went to his servant (260) and said: "Let us not stay here, we must ride off, the time has not yet come to return home as I had thought previously." (265) He immediately said goodbye [to the host]. Onward they traveled. Honestly, I tell you, the further the man went on his journey, the less he heard of that (270) which his heart so desired. Thus he rode all over the country until he had spent thousands of gold coins that he had in his purse, and finally he had only a little money left. (275)

Then he took lodging in a large and extended city. There he selected an inn-keeper who was mighty and also rich. It seemed to him that the life of the latter and his wife (280) was equal. He thought that he had [at last] found two souls in one body in this woman and her husband. He was very pleased with their life [together]. (285) He studied them carefully to determine whether he could observe anything to the contrary. He was even ready to go home because he had found two married people who were unified (290) in a harmonious marriage. Each loved the other loyally without any doubt.

When the innkeeper noticed that the guest wanted to depart, (295) he said: "Dear guest, I like you very much. You display a courtly and decent behavior. It seems to me that you are looking for an adventure. Let me know what it might be. I am a man here (300) of such family connections and power that I might easily help you in this town and in its surroundings. If you have any pressing issue, then let me know it in confidence; (305) no one will find out about it."

The guest answered him politely: "I will tell you my secret intention. I am pursuing a strange adventure. At home I have a lovely wife (310) who does everything according to my wishes. Each of us appreciates what the other does. We agree fully. But there is one problem with her; (315) she is really too miserly. This grieves me considerably. Truly, I tell you: at home I enjoy much power but I rode away (320) and went to distant lands. I have spent probably thousands of gold coins because I cannot find a woman and her husband who are entirely unified in their minds. (325) Instead I encounter nothing but bickering and fighting wherever I have traveled. The one pulls this way, the other the opposite way. I had intended not to return home (330) until I found two married people of whom I could observe no disagreement between them. I have been searching for this for more than six years now. (335) Only now do I realize that I have discovered this ideal couple in you and your wife. I do not observe anything between you but that you are friendly to each other (340), both day and night. I am so happy and joyful about it. Therefore I have prepared to return home to my wife and my house; (345) after all, I have been away for a long time."

The host then said to the guest: "The trouble you describe with your wife it is very little. I will tell you of my heart-felt suffering (350) in complete confidence, if you keep quiet and do not tell anyone about it. Promise me this right here, because I do not want to let anyone [else] know about it. (355) The guest did not hesitate and promised him that he would not divulge this account to anyone because he was loyal and honest.

The host then took his guest and led him into his house (360) down to a deep and expansive cellar. In a hidden corner was a wide room with stone walls that the host opened for his guest. A large peasant lived in it (365) who was terrible to look at, strong, and evil. He was locked with a strong and solid chain so that he could not leave. He stood there as if a stormy breeze (370) had disheveled his hair, and he appeared to be very threatening. When the guest saw the peasant he asked the host: "This is a most strange matter.(375) What is the meaning of this frightful peasant, whom you keep a prisoner?"

The host responded without hesitation: "Dear guest, I will tell you how my life truly is. (380) Pay close attention. I originate from a good family, and so does my wife. We might well be the most noble family here in the city, be assured of that, (385) both in terms of our birth and our wealth. But my wife does not comport herself as is would befitting her, because she is filled with unchaste desire [literally: full of unchastity]. This lack of chastity drove her around the city (390) and cast shame on her family. My honor was also robbed from me, and I had to suffer for her evil nature. Both old and young deemed me to be too weak because of my wife's failing. (395) When I realized her deficiency and that she did not intend to combat it, I acted as one who commands dignity and honor. I rode to a distant country (400) where no one knew me. I found this strong peasant there. With the help of my friends and servants I forcefully kidnapped him. This happened all in secret, (405) and no one heard or saw whereto he had disappeared. I transported him secretly here into my house without any difficulties. Here he has to stay a prisoner (410) as long as my wife lives. She visits him whenever she wants to do her evil thing. He makes love to her until she is satisfied (415) and has no further demands.

"Everyone assumes that she has truly improved, so now she is appreciated and valued publicly. But my honor is deeply hurt, (420) in secret and silently. The same wine and food that I enjoy every day I personally bring to the peasant for his dinner. (425) I take better care of him, by my honor, than of myself in order that he may sleep with my wife so that she will be sexually satisfied and does not look for the pleasure of sex elsewhere, (430) as she used to do. That brought shame and disgrace upon me in the past. I tell you truly, this torture I have endured for ten years. (435) During that time my wife has not had sex with any other man. Dear guest, look at the children whom I have under my care. Everyone assumes (440) they are my own. This is a cause of great pain for me because they are the peasant's offspring, all six of my children."

When the guest heard these words, (445) he was deeply horrified. The host's suffering grieved him badly. The latter then spoke to him again: "I advise you, honestly, do not stay away any longer (450) from your virtuous and good wife. You behave badly toward her, indeed. She does not deserve to be treated this way because she is not guilty of any disloyalty. Her miserliness cannot be reprimanded. (455) Believe me if you intend to travel around the country, you will squander your wealth and lose it entirely before you find (460) what you seeking.

"No one is completely perfect. The devil likes to sow his seeds [of discontent] among married people, which makes it impossible (465) for them to live together without any strife."

The guest immediately followed the host's advice. He decided to ride home as the host had recommended to him. In friendship he said goodbye, (470) but he was very sad [for him]. He gave one horse in payment for food to make the journey home. The servant had to walk on foot. (475) The noble man thus rode off and soon they both got home. The honorable and chaste wife was happy with her husband's return. From then on he no longer opposed (480) her parsimonious lifestyle.

Der Mutterturm (Mother's Tower), Landsberg am Lech

Often he thought of the places where he had been of the drinking vessel and of the giant peasant (485) held by chains. When he carefully considered everything he realized that the lives that he and his wife enjoyed were free of shame and suffering. (490) He accepted when she became angry with him because of his excessive generosity [literally: carried the crown of generosity] and tolerated her chiding.

Therefore let me give you this advice. (495) Every good man ought to disregard little shortcomings of his wife if he cannot discover any other blemish in her character except for her miserliness. (500) He should consign himself to it and not cause her any pain or aggravate her because it is the least shortcoming from which a woman might suffer. (505) More I am not going to tell you.

No. 9: *The Canon and the Cobbler*

Now let me tell you a new adventure that took place only recently in the splendid city of Augsburg. The pretty wife of a shoemaker/cobbler (5) was in love with a man and felt strongly about him in her heart. He was a clever canon.[1] He loved her very much.[2]

One day that woman (10) had, as her heart desired, invited him to her home. This took place in the month of May. The servants prepared a bath for them both in a large tub. (15) The naked man sat down in it, and with him the sweet woman. The tub was well protected from view by a curtain of silk, so that no one could look inside. (20) Now, the woman had a rather simple-minded husband about whom she worried little, even though he was home at the same time. He sat in his workshop (25) and busily pursued his job. He worked dutifully, and his wife was not afraid of him because he represented no danger to her. The tub was placed openly (30) in front of the elegant chamber. Joyfully the man sat there with the fine woman.

The husband came from his workshop and wanted to enter the room (35) to get more leather for his work. When the smart woman noticed that, she peeked out from the tub and said to him without any fear: (40) "Come here, my dear husband! A worthy canon is sitting here next to me in the big tub. He is entirely naked. Come here and take a look. (45) I swear to you by my honor that is the full truth." The shoemaker responded to his wife in a friendly manner: "Spare me your mockery, (50) because I truly know that no one is sitting next to you. I have other things to do than to look behind the curtain before the tub." (55) The woman did not let it go; she swore by her loyalty that the situation [as described] was true, as she said before. The fool [of a husband] approached the tub (60) and wanted to look inside. There the worthy canon sitting in the tub felt great fear and lost all joy. Now, as the husband approached the curtain, (65) the wife scooped up a handful of water and splashed it into his eyes so that he could no longer see anything. For a while he was blinded. He began to laugh and said: (70) "Indeed, I knew beforehand that you would not spare me your mockery and your playful manner, which you practice all the time. But now at least I have the upper hand (75) having gotten away from you. If you had gotten hold of me, you

---

[1] A canon is a cleric serving as one of the priests and administrators in the chapter of a cathedral or a collegiate church.

[2] Literally: "He loved her beautiful (or worthy) body."

would have wet my clothing. Now I'll let this be without anger (80) since I did not suffer any damage. You are the loser and I am the winner."

When his wife heard his words, she made a gesture as if she wanted to grab him, (85) but he fled far away from her and left behind a pleasant situation for the two people. The canon spoke to the woman: "I had a sweat bath here. Never in my whole life (90) have I sweated more in a bath than today. If the masseur[3] of the bathhouse had spied me here, as almost happened, he would have beaten me up, (95) causing me great pain. It would have been a disaster for me. He would have demonstrated his skill toward me, a man in love, because he knows how to shave people. (100) He would have shaved me without lather. How could I be recompensed by you, my dear lady? It seems to me that I did not benefit from your bath, (105), surely as if you had poured scalding water that would have melted me away."

The canon then left the woman. He wondered (110) how he could cause the woman worry and fear as she had caused him. He was a really clever man and planned right away (115) to organize the Widergeltlingen sorrow [idiomatic phrase], not far from Türkheim.[4] Quickly the canon repaid the woman for his sweat bath.

One day he snared her (120) from morning until noon, since she usually got up and left her husband behind in order to go to morning mass. She visited the canon, (125) who was laying in his bed. Lovingly she lay next to him. When the man saw that, he quickly called his scribe [= secretary] and whispered into his ear (130) to call for the shoemaker. "Do not allow any refusal; he should bring with him three pairs of shoelasts."[5] The scribe quickly went (135) to the shoemaker and asked him to come, as his lord had ordered. The shoemaker was ready and did not linger. Soon he entered (140) the canon's house, who called from his room and asked the shoemaker to enter. He greeted him. He had covered the woman's head (145) and exposed her feet. He took one of the feet and showed it the shoemaker, saying: "Find a shoe last [model of a human foot for the preparation of a shoe] (150) that seems to fit to this foot and make two wonderful shoes for this sweet young woman. I will pay you well for it. The shoemaker said to the canon, (155) looking at the feet: "I have here three pairs of lasts that are too large and do not fit these feet. At home I certainly have (160) two fitting shoe lasts that I have made for my wife's shoes. I swear this young woman has two feet (165) just like my wife, be assured of that. If I did not know my wife better, I would immediately believe that these were her feet.[6] However, I am sure that she is at home (170) working on something that is of more profit for me than spending time with you. Otherwise, that would be bad news. Therefore, my dear lord,

---

[3] I acknowledge Simmons's better word choice here and borrow it for my purpose.

[4] Metaphorical: the town of Pay Back, not far from the city of Cunning.

[5] These are wooden models for shoemaking.

[6] Literally he says "legs" but really means "feet."

(175) I will make for this young woman [daughter] two very pretty shoes." The canon joyfully said: "Do that, my dear friend." He then called his scribe, (180) who came in quickly. He said: "Take the shoemaker to my good cellar and give him a glass of white wine to drink."

They both left the room. (185) The woman lay there feeling her heart aches. They both were now even with each other; the sweat bath was repaid in a clever fashion without any threats. (190) While the husband stayed in the cellar, the canon arranged to have the woman get away from the house. She went home without fear as if she had come from church. (195) She cleverly took the distaff in her hand, sat down, and began to spin. Soon the good husband entered through the door and said: "My dear wife, (200) I almost was suspicious about you, but since I find you here, my stupid idea has disappeared."

He told the wife the entire story from beginning to end (205) — how, without suspecting anything, he had seen in the canon's room a young woman laying with him in bed, for whom he was told to measure the feet for shoes. (210) He said: "The young woman offered me two snow-white feet from the bed to my hand. I could conclude nothing else but that that young woman (215) had two delicate and fine feet that were just like yours. They were pretty and also small. If I had not known that you were at home (220) I would have assumed that you had gone to the priest." When the woman heard his words, she felt profound anger in her heart toward her husband. She turned to him wrathfully: (225) "You might have lost your mind looking into my eyes." The wife began to cry violently and said: "You insult me so much without any guilt on my part, by my honor. (230) That will pain me for eternity. Truly, I will never forgive you that." The husband became deeply frightened that he had caused his wife such grief. He begged her to be of good cheer (235) and said: "Upon my loyalty, I spoke those words without evil intention. I well know that I have a virtuous wife without any cunning. I beg you deeply, (240) let me regain your grace. I will make up for my fault however you can think, since I must rightly repent for having impugned you with my words." (245) The woman barely granted him the favor to regain her grace.[7]

Even today you can find many a man who suffers injustice and has to repent to his wife (250) when she more properly should do it herself. When the husband chastises her evil actions, she quickly finds a way with her smart strategies to make him accept that he was at fault. (255) Thus many a husband is misused by his wife. To tell the truth, here on earth many men (260) are often deceived by women. That's true and not a lie. The men are truly martyrs. With this the story comes to an end.

---

[7] Simmons reads the adverb "hart" as "firmly," whereas I interpret it as "barely," because the wife plays hardball with her husband.

No. 10: *The Pants Left Behind*

A noble lady once invited a clever young man into her chamber. Her heart was filled with love for him. He lay in bed with her (5) and did wonderful loving things. But their joy was suddenly destroyed by the lord of the house, her husband, who entered the building. (10) He approached the chamber, so the young man had to run out the room, using a ladder outside, by which he managed to escape. (15) But he had to leave his pants behind on a chest in front of the bed. The husband entered the room and immediately discovered the pants. He picked them up (20) and asked: "Who brought these here?" The woman quickly made up something to explain their presence to him. She was quick-witted and not dumb. She grabbed him by the collar (25) and shook him back and forth, swaying his whole body. His wife then said, in a serious tone: "Speak these words: 'pants, pants,' my dear husband!" He replied: "You might have lost your mind, (30) because you are frightening, shaking, and choking me so rabidly." She said: "Your words are pointless because you are not saying 'pants, pants.'" She did not stop, she shook him even more, (35) shouting: "Say, 'pants, pants,' and do not stop!" She did this for a long time until she forced the man to say: "Pants, pants." "This way you will recover (40) from your illness," said the wife. "With the pants I chase away the headaches and the evil pain that have bothered you for a long time until now. (45) Just as the pants can disappear from here without any problems, so all your problems and sickness will go away for good and won't afflict you again." (50) With these words she threw the pants out of the window into the yard, where the fine young man was standing. He picked them up happily and put them on again. (55) Joyfully he ran away.

Once this had happened, the woman spoke to her husband: "You must be thankful forever because I have rescued you. (60) Now the evil spirit will never be able to touch you again. Whoever suffers from the same illness will not find help and will not recover (65) except by being frightened unexpectedly and without hesitation. I borrowed those pants and did not tell you anything about them. But your illness was thereby chased away (70) and will never return, because I have frightened you mightily."

The husband thanked her very much. As a reward he gave her a [wool] coat, a dress, and a good fur coat. (75) Nevertheless, the man was not well-protected because he was thoroughly deceived. To tell the truth, I am not sure whether the "therapy" (80) caused him more hurt and suffering.

Any woman can deceive her husband easily, as has often happened [even] to those who are wise. (85) Now, we [ordinary people] are void of wisdom and not equal to them. For that reason we can certainly be deceived by women. That's not a lie. (90) The strong Samson and the wise Solomon, as well as the mighty King David, were equally deceived and tricked by women. (95) It is an old story: we can all be easily hoodwinked by women here on earth. (100) If by the skill of her nature a cunning and pretty woman managed to defeat the wise man Aristotle, convincing him to let her ride him with spurs on and thus tame him, (105) certainly no one should be angry with clever women because they deceive all of us without fail. I have learned well that this is common (110) from wise men to fools. Hence we do not really lose when we experience the same misfortune of being deceived by women [throw us over the rope].[1] (115) More I am not going to tell you.

---

[1] An idiomatic phrase for which there is no equivalent in English. It is documented as a proverb used by some preachers, such as Geiler von Kaisersberg (1445–1510); see http://woerterbuchnetz.de/Wander/?sigle=Wander&mode=Vernetzung&lemid=WS01964 (see no. 25) (last accessed on Sept. 5, 2014).

No. 11: *Three Clever Women, B*

I believe that no honorable person is more deceived and cheated here on earth by means of cunning and clever strategies than a husband by his wife. (5) I will tell you of an adventure that I remember.

There were worthy peasant women whom we all know well: the first was called Lady Jüt, (10) the other is called Lady Hiltgart, and the third I will not exclude and name her right away as well: she is named Lady Mächthilt [Mechthild?]. They prepared themselves to go to a pleasant city. (15) They took eggs with them to sell at the market. They agreed without fail (20) to divide equally the money that mighty God would grant them for the eggs. On that day they sold the eggs for seven farthings [coinage]. (25) Each one received two, but then bickering broke out among the women over the last farthing. (30) They argued for a long time, because each one wanted it. Lady Hiltgart said: "Now listen to what I am thinking. I have a good idea (35), which pleases me on my life, that whoever among us can deceive her husband in the best way with her clever trick (40) should receive the seventh farthing without any complaints." These words pleased them well, to tell the truth. They promised each other (45) to keep the pledge and not to change anything.

When Lady Hiltgart came home, she noticed immediately that her husband had come home from the field and was sitting at the table, (50) eating a large bowl of porridge. She went into the house [room] and cleverly began to deceive the good man, who was called Berthold. (55) She was neither loyal to him nor did she love him. She sighed heavily when she came near him and pretended to be severely sick. She said: "Alas, what great lament, (60) I have to die! No one can help me in that except you, my dear husband. If you demonstrate your loyalty to me right now (65), I will become well and healthy immediately. But if you leave me alone in my misery, I will have to kiss bitter death, right now before your eyes." The husband said: (70) "My dear wife, what ails you also hurts me. How may I help you? Let me know right away. I love you so much that no pain would be too great (75) for me to suffer on your behalf, certainly, so that your sickness comes to an end."

Hiltgart said to her husband: "You have a really rotten tooth (80) in the middle of your mouth. I suffer this pain because the evil smell from your mouth causes me to be ill and so I must die before my time. (85) Truly, I tell you, no other medicine could help me effectively against death but that you allow the tooth to be pulled, whereupon (90) I shall still enjoy many days of my life."

The man said to his wife: "This is strange news. Until now I have never had any tooth aches. (95) God has blessed me with strong and healthy teeth." The woman then behaved even worse than before. The man was a real fool. (100) He believed that she might be in the thrall of death. She made that clear by her mimicry of suffering the greatest pain. The man strongly believed in his heart (105) that he had a smelling tooth. He would have sworn a hundred oaths on that. Thus he became a fool because of his wife's deception.

He had a farmhand who was rather carefree (110) and felt great love for the wife. He provided her with much fun. They both were infatuated with each other. He returned [at that moment] from the field, as was his duty, driving the plow cart, (115) while the couple were suffering. He stepped into the room, and his master begged him urgently, saying; "My dear farmhand, help your lady (120) so that she does not pass away from a sudden death. I have in my mouth a tooth that is rotten. Pull it out for me, (125) so that my wife's suffering is overcome."

The farmhand immediately prepared to do that on behalf of the wife. He tied the peasant tightly to a chair, (130) making it impossible for him to move. The lady then handed him huge pliers. The peasant was unhappy when he saw the large pliers. (135) He suffered this pain willingly on behalf of his wife. The farmhand operated on him in a masterly fashion. He grabbed the left jaw and pulled out (140) a strong, healthy tooth with the pliers. This made blood stream from the foolish man's mouth. He had never experienced greater pain in all his life (145). But in truth, I tell you, the wife was not content with that. She arranged to deceive the peasant even more.

Now you might like to hear the following. (150) She screamed: "Alas, my sorrow! I have to choose bitter death, the pain increases in me. Truly, I have to tell you that." She said to the farmhand: (155) "That was not the right tooth that you pulled out of the left side of his mouth with the pliers. Pay close attention, the tooth that threatens my life (160) is located on the right side of his mouth." The farmhand picked up the pliers again, took them quickly in hand, and the peasant had to suffer even more pain. It went so far (165) that another good tooth was pulled from his mouth, this time from the right side. He fainted from pain; he could neither hear nor see as a result of that torture (170) and turned very pale. The woman noticed this, but she wanted to deceive him even further. She said to the farmhand: "Quickly, ask the priest to come to my husband (175) so that he can tell him his sins in confession, since death is approaching him."

The priest hurriedly arrived, and when the woman saw him, (180) she complained to him about her sorrows. She cried and screamed excessively as does one who has an honest reason for it in her heart. The peasant gave a full confession (185), because his mind was so tortured that he truly believed he was dying. The priest gave him God's blessing and then left. The woman sat in front of the good man (190) and cried openly so that the peasant himself believed that things were worse than they really were. She did all this with the purpose of deceiving him even further. (195) Soon she brought candles and put them into his hands. She said: "God has sent His messenger in this hour. The soul is departing from the mouth (200) at this moment. Oh Lord God, come here [without being asked] and receive this beautiful soul and take it to God's throne, where it should rest in eternity. (205) May God's grace be with you, my dear husband!"

When she finished speaking, the woman quickly brought out a cloth and covered it over him. The peasant himself believed that his soul had left him. (210) The woman screamed with a loud voice: "Woe is me in this misery! My dear husband has passed away. Oh dear, my heart's beloved! I can never stop lamenting because your loyalty [dedication/love] was so great (215) that you locked me in your heart; I will have to grieve for eternity whenever I think of you. Woe is me, my dear Berthold, I have always loved you. (220) I will feel sadness forever over having lost you in such a way."

The news that Lady Hiltgart had been widowed spread everywhere in the village. (225) She diligently locked both the back and the front of the house so that she could place her husband on a bier without a cover. She skillfully placed a plain cloth over him. (230) The peasant peaked through it, looking at what was being done with him. Once she finished all preparations, she unlocked the front door. Lady Jüt and Lady Mächthilt, along with the neighbors, (235) then entered the house. They mourned the sad woman, lamenting that she in her beauty and respectability was bereft of her husband. But Lady Mächthilt (240) as well as Lady Jüt secretly recognized how and in what manner the entire event had transpired, but they did not dare say anything about it; instead they left the house with the other people. (245)

No one stayed in the house but the woman and her farmhand, which pleased them both. The woman sat down next to the bier. She had a crazy idea in her mind. (250) She lamented the husband's death and entrusted herself to the farmhand, saying: "Now you have to console me, and then I will submit myself to you, (255) to die with you or revive." The farmhand promised immediately to support her. He embraced her tenderly and placed her underneath himself (260) because he worried little about the husband. He lay between her legs and made love to her without concern. The peasant looked out of the bier because his face was not covered. (265) With his own eyes he saw that they slept with each other and played the game of love. He called out: "Farmhand Heintz, if I were still alive, as I certainly was this morning, (270) this shameful behavior [by you] would cause me heart-felt pain. I would not avoid getting my revenge, even if I might be stabbed to death by you. Now I have to let it go, (275) since I can no longer hurt anyone, stricken by grim death, which has felled me and torn apart my limbs" (280).

Enough of that, let us leave this story as is. Now, fine Lady Hiltgart deceived her husband equally well. But to tell the truth, I am not so sure (285) whether she deserved to receive the seventh farthing as a reward. Clearly, I cannot decide that. Now, I want to let you know how Lady Jüt (290) cheated on and deceived her husband, who was called Conrad. When it turned evening, the peasant Conrad had learned the news that peasant Berthold was dead. (295) Lady Jüt was also fully informed. She ordered enough mead and wine, as she well knew how to do, to make her husband so full of wine (300) and so completely drunk that he did not know what he was doing. As a result of his extreme drunkenness he fell deeply asleep on the bed next to his pretty wife. (305) She did not linger but got a good shaving knife and shaved her husband right away, and so made an unordained priest out of that monkey. (310) Thereafter she put him to bed. Lady Jüt lay down next to him. He slept deeply the entire night.

When day broke and the bells were rung, (315) Lady Hiltgart arranged to have her husband carried to the church. What else shall I tell you? Lady Jüt softly shook her husband who, was lying in bed, (320) and cleverly woke him: "Quick, get up, Sir Heinrich," she said to her husband. This was the name of the priest, who had left for a journey at that time. (325) She woke her husband in a smart manner, without making any noise, pretending that he was the proper priest. He had a bad headache (330) from heavy drinking and did not notice his wife's kiss. She poked him in the side: "Get up, my dear lord! Do you not hear the sound of the bells? (335) Truly, today you are sleeping too long. Get up and receive payment on behalf of the peasant Berthold, whose funeral service is today in the church." The peasant Conrad responded: (340) "What do you mean? What illusion makes you think that I am suddenly the priest? You know very well that I do not know how to read." (345)

Lady Jüt said to her husband: "Why do you say that, Sir Heinrich? Go to the church and take care of the corpse at the holy altar and offer the funeral mass for him. (350) That would be much better, honestly, than to keep lying here." The peasant Conrad said: "I do not know what to make of your words. (355) You enjoy making fun of me. You call me the priest Heinrich, but I am much more like the peasant Conrad." Lady Jüt answered him thusly: "On my honor, I swear: (360) you are my lord, the priest Heinrich. Touch your head and you will know right away that I tell you the truth." (365) He touched his head and discovered that he had a tonsure, as a priest should. He said: "Now I recognize (370) that I truly am a priest. Yet in my mind I think this is not the case because I am completely ignorant. I do not know how to read. (375)

Lady Jüt did not accept this excuse and said: "Go to church immediately; God does not allow you to shirk your responsibility. As soon as you will up to the altar, you will know how to read the book." (380) The peasant Conrad believed her. He quickly went to the church, accompanied by Lady Jüt. She placed him in front of the altar and put on his mass vestments. (385) She said: "Stand here quietly until the people arrive. It is still a little too early." The peasant Conrad stood there in front of the altar as if he were the priest (he might get white hair for his worries). (390) When the people had arrived, no one really recognized that he was the peasant Conrad. He stood there in the priest's vestment, (395) having been badly deceived by Lady Jüt, which was her great success. But let us pause here.

I do not wish to wait much longer to talk about Lady Mächthilt, (400) how she shamed her husband who was called peasant Seifrid. At night when he went to sleep, Lady Mächthilt, without being noticed, secretly took away all his clothing from the good man. (405) When the night ended and the bright day began, she woke him and said: "You should not rest in bed any longer. (410) We both must go to church. The priest wants to say mass. Sadly, peasant Bertholt is dead. Get up, dear husband, let us bring our devotional sacrifice. (415) You know very well that he was our good friend."

The peasant Seifrid heard what she said and quickly got up from bed. "I cannot find my clothing here," (420) he told his wife. She answered: "On my honor, you are already dressed; stay behind no longer. Otherwise we will be late for the service. (425) The mass is almost over by now. Go, do not say anything further." The peasant Seifrid answered: "My goodness, I don't want to go naked to church. They will all mock me. (430) Stop making all that noise, hand me my clothing right away!" His wife responded wrathfully: (435) "Truly, you have lost your mind and are blind with eyes open. Ask everyone in the church; they will not be able to say anything but that they truly see you (440) standing there with your clothes on."

Lady Mächthilt did not budge; she swore to him that this was the truth so often and so strongly that the man no longer dared to speak against her. (445) He accepted the idea and would have sworn a hundred oaths that his body was beautifully clothed. His evil wife made him think so. He entered the church (450) stark naked together with his wife.

Peasant Conrad stood at the altar and peasant Bertholt lay there on the bier. Peasant Seifrid went up to the altar without any clothing. (455) He wanted to place his sacrifice there on behalf of his friend, peasant Bertholt. He grabbed at his balls and thought that they were his purse, (460) which he wanted to open. He looked for the two strings, but he could not find them. Truly he had intended, to take out money for the offering from the purse. (465) Lady Mächthilt approached him while he stood there very confused to open the purse for him. She pulled out a sharp knife and said: "You really are useless; (470) you cannot help yourself. Let me see your good purse, maybe I can open it for you." She cut off his balls. (475) The peasant Seifrid felt enormous pain because he lost a good body part. Peasant Seifrid screamed so loudly that it echoed in the church. He ran out, making noise (480) as if he had lost his mind. Filled with rage, he loudly wished his wife dead.

When the peasant Conrad heard that, he quickly ran away from the altar. (485) He also shouted: "My wife has badly deceived me; the devil be her reward!" He also ran out of the church. Outside he found (490) peasant Seifrid screaming wildly, walking up and down as if he were a mad dog because he suffered such a serious wound. He howled as loudly and deeply as a cow. (495) Peasant Conrad also raged. Then they ran away over the pasture into the forest, both driven mad. The ladies Jüt and Mächthilt had (500) created all that for the seventh farthing.

The entire congregation; both young and old, tall and short, observed these events. (505) They really did not understand what had happened to those two men. They wanted to find out what it was all about. Honestly, everyone ran out of the church; no one stayed behind. (510) Then the peasant Berthold on the bier screamed out in a loud voice: "Why am I laying here? I have been deceived by my disloyal wife, but I do not know how. (515) May the devil enter her !" With these words he jumped up. It was difficult for him to walk. He ran to the people outside and shouted angrily: (520) "Where is the evil Lady Hiltgart? I will not wait to give her my reward. She must lose her life right here at my own hands; (525) no one can help her." The people became very frightened— one ran here, the other there; they were all afraid of the "dead" man and escaped from him, (530) with no one staying behind.

One could get gray hair from hearing [seeing] this story. The peasant Berthold thought about what to do. Then he saw peasant Seifrid and peasant Conrad running over the pasture, (535) filled with pain, so he followed them. He wanted to understand what had happened to both of them. (540) He rushed after them into the forest.

Now, let us forget about these fools running into the woods, until they realize that they are all acting drunk (545) and blind with their eyes open, recognize what happened and run home again and let it all be, forgetting all their pain. (550)

But I would like to know which woman better deceived and hoodwinked her husband. Him who could tell me that, I would truly consider a wise man. (555) She who had achieved her goal would certainly deserve the seventh farthing. I myself cannot decide. Herewith ends the story.

No. 12: *The Tithe on Love*

I have told you before that women skillfully engage in schemes by which simple-minded men are often and repeatedly hoodwinked. (5) You rarely find a woman on earth who does not command that kind of cunning. The art of deception is second nature to women, because they are pleased when they mislead men (10) with their plans. Wherever I look around the world, in cities, villages, and all over the countryside, I do not know of any woman who is a simpleton, (15) who does not possess intelligence, except for one, upon whom I have based this account. I want to tell about her, who was beautiful, well-mannered, (20) plain, full of virtue. There were no evil thoughts in her, and she displayed complete loyalty. There was no evil in her mind. She was fashionable, lovely, (25) and possessed much wealth. She lived in a pleasant village married to a well-mannered, virtuous peasant.

The priest [in the village] developed great love (30) for this woman yet did not dare to open his heart to her, because he well knew that she led a virtuous, good life (35) well protected from all evilness. It happened that the entire peasant community and the priest, together with that lady, spent time in the inn during Shrovetide, (40) having a good time, as one always tends to have then. The priest took notice. When a break occurred during the drinking, (45) he took the woman aside and sat quietly with her. He whispered to her and said: "Dear lady, I want to tell you a concern I have secretly carried for a long time (50) in my heart. Looking at your life it seems to me that you are God's friend. You always give to God what belongs to Him. (55) Your sacrifice is pure and good, your alms are worthy. Now, if your virtues were complete and you gave your tithe fully, not burdening your soul with the same old sin, (60) you would gain God's grace in fully, eternal heaven. Otherwise you will be lost and condemned (65) to suffer hellish pain forever." The woman became deeply frightened and said: "Lord, teach me how I can achieve access to heaven, since I believed (70) that I gave my tithe to the fullest extent."

The priest responded: "I tell you that you have not done so. I should receive the tithe of your love, which you have denied me so far. (75) You have failed in that regard so God is displeased with you." The woman, not suspecting anything responded: "No one has told me about that before. I regret from the bottom of my heart (80) to have acted against God. I will be most happy to do penance according to your advice and your teaching." The priest spoke further to the woman: "You must keep quiet about this (85) to your husband and think for yourself what you are obliged to give me from the love-making over the past half year, (90) which is owed to me. Then I will forgo the debt from what occurred before, and you will be absolved from then on. God's grace will be bestowed on you (95) because you did not know that it was a wrong."

The woman was free of any devious thoughts and spoke most innocently: "My husband has, during the past half year (100), lain with me about thirty times and made love with me." Thereupon the good priest said: "Three times of love-making are the right number for the tithe belonging to me; (105) those actions certainly belong to me. If you let me have them, as I ought to receive them, then tomorrow I will come early in the morning when your husband is working in the field (110) and will take the tithe from you." Without any second thought the woman said: "I will happily grant you whatever is owed to you."

When the next morning came, (115) the peasant prepared himself and drove to the field. Then the priest came to the woman's house. She welcomed him kindly. (120) He told the pretty woman: "Grant me my tithe, or you will have lost God's grace." The woman feared God's wrath and did not want to fight about it. (125) She let him collect the tithe on the plowed field. The priest lay with the woman until noon and took her love three times. (130) He was fully granted his tithe.

Then the priest left filled with joy, since he had succeeded in his plan. Just as he stepped out of the door, (135) the peasant came driving back from the field. The priest could not hide from the peasant, who wondered (140) why the priest was in his house. He said to his wife: "Tell me, what has the priest done here?" (145). The woman was not a cunning person and did not think anything evil. She openly told her husband: "I tell you honestly, he told me in truth (150) and warned me as a loyal person that I had acted against God, having not given him a tithe as owed, wherefore I would have to face punishment in hell. That was a great worry for me. (155) If you had been loyal and honest, as you ought to be for God's sake, you should have pointed out to me a long time ago that I owed the priest (160) the tithe of my love. However, he urged me never to forget paying the tithe again as I did before, and then I would be released (165) from the accrued interest. Thus I will regain God's grace. For that reason I paid my debt with love-making three times, which he took from me (170) today."

When the husband heard her words, they pleased him little. He said: "You should no longer give this tithe on love (175) or I will kill you. This time I will forgive you, but it must never happen again." "Since I have done wrong," said the wife to her husband, (180) "I will never do it again. Please forgive me now." The man promised his wife and said without anger: "Now, do not tell the priest (185) that I learned about this story. I won't let it pass; he will have to do penance for me." The woman said: "I will help you (190) with whatever plan you come up with; we will punish this dumb priest, causing him great embarrassment to my heart's delight."[1]

The peasant then made a plan; (195) he told his wife that he wanted to organize a big festive dinner with plenty of food and strong wine, inviting the respectable priest. He bought two good jugs. (200) The one he filled with wine of the best possible quality; the other jug which had a big, wide hole, he put away. (205) He told his wife to pee into it without delay; thus he intended to hoodwink the priest. She peed into it until it was full.

The next day, when it was time to eat (210) the priest came to them without fear because he had been invited and he felt happy and cheerful, as every lover feels who comes to see his beloved. (215) He had in his secret heart many joys and delight, love without sorrow, and much entertainment. The priest was seated at the table. They served him venison and fish (220) and everything else as was to be expected. They took good care of him. The priest glanced lovingly at his dear mistress often, (225) which the husband clearly observed but pretended not to notice.

Once the table was cleared and the food carried away because they had had enough, (230) the lord of the house said to the priest: "Lord, now I will get us very good wine after the meal; the table wine is still too fresh. If this seems good for you, (235) let us have a sweet wine." Those words pleased the priest, but the peasant had no loyalty toward him for good reason. He ordered his wife (240) to bring in the big jug to them. She quickly fulfilled her husband's command. The jug was brought to them, (245) which the peasant noted. He offered it to the priest and said: "Lord, drink this sweet Italian wine, which derives from a good grape." The priest took the jug, (250) which had a wide opening on top. The husband praised the wine so much that the priest took a huge swig without concern. Indeed, he swallowed much at once. (255) The drink shot down his throat, so much that it spilled over. A great struggle erupted in his throat, and he threw up (260) whatever he had eaten and drunk. Everything went out of him in a straight line since he spit out all. Nothing stayed in his stomach. Then he said: "That was an evil drink. (265) My lungs, liver, and intestines are all badly shaken. I will never recover from that." The peasant responded: "What happened to you? Truly, I must say (270) on my oath that this was good and clear wine from which you have recently taken the tithe. (275) The vineyard is also perfect; I have worked in it well, and as a reward I have received love and happiness. It belongs to me and cannot be loaned out. (280) No one has a right to work in it, neither lay people nor clerics, only me, let me tell you that! In my lifetime, no tithe ever has to be paid for it. (285) He who tries to get more out of it will reap such a fruit that he will fall into such deep suffering and sorrow that death might seem better for him." (290)

---

[1] There is no clear explanation how the wife suddenly manages to see through the priest's evil plan, since the narrator had portrayed her as such a naive person.

When the priest heard those words, he became very frightened. He greatly feared the peasant's wrath because he lost his favor. Urgently he begged him (295) and spoke in friendly terms: "Dear peasant, what I have done, please forgive me and no longer dwell on it; consider your own honor. (300) You are the host and I am your guest. Whatever you might do against me now would be against the honor of your house. I promise you on my honor that it will never happen again. (305) I will be your servant forever, and I tell you frankly that the guilt was all mine. Your wife is truly virtuous and pure. (310) I deceived her and lied to her foolishly so that she became my victim, without fault and quite innocently. (315) Do not punish her nor treat her worse than before, because she has done this without evil intent."

Because the priest spoke well, the husband forgave (320) what had been committed against him. All previous guilt was forgotten and a steady friendship was re-established. The priest was always ready to help the peasant (325) and never again did anything to hurt him. Thus ends our story.

No. 13: *The Revenge of the Husband*

Once there lived a bold and high-minded knight in a strong castle regularly attended the court where he looked for service, (5) expending himself strongly. He entertained himself with jousting in tournaments where he achieved his best. He was married to a beautiful woman, (10) whom the priest also loved; both were infatuated with each other.[1]

One evening after the knight had left the priest was lying with her and enjoyed making love to her. (15) The priest said, in a polite manner, to his dear mistress: "I beg you, my dear lady, grant me one favor that you will honor me particularly. (20) If you do that, I will believe that your heart is loyal and that you love me more than all other men." She sweetly responded: (25) "Lord, whatever you might ask me, you will be granted. My heart, my mind, and my will all urge me to offer you my service. (30) The priest quietly told her: "So, I beg you, when my lord [the knight] comes home, remember our oath of loyalty, which binds us together. (35) I ask you to get two molars from your husband's mouth; you will thereby comply with my wish." The woman promised him that.

When the knight had returned home (40) to his wife and wanted to hug her, as he normally did, the woman turned away from him and acted as if he were disgusting. (45) The knight said: "Why do you lean away from me? Who has caused you pain? Before you usually demonstrated a friendly behavior toward me. Tell me, what is wrong with you? (50) I will help you, if it is in my power." She said: "Truly, I tell you, my dear lord, what I suffer from is that you have a tooth in your mouth that smells very badly. (55) I have suffered a long time from that foul smell, but I cannot tolerate it any longer. I will die a premature death unless you have the tooth pulled out right here. (60) Then the bad smell will disappear from your mouth, and I will happily be close to you until the end of my life. Otherwise my life will be miserable, if you do not get rid of that tooth, (65) which causes terrible breath."

The knight felt badly when he heard her words. He called for a barber [surgeon] who was a master in his art. He did this out of love for his wife (70) because he was loyally committed to her. He believed that she was committed to him and could be trusted fully, as she ought to be, but actually she was enamored with the priest, who was her lover. (75)

---

[1] The original sounds rather funny and deserves to be rendered literally, at least here in the footnote: "They were not disinclined to each other."

When the barber arrived at the knight's castle, the lord told him openly: "Dear master, grope here in the left side of my mouth (80) where I have a molar, as far as I know, that might be the worst[2] in my mouth. Pull it out immediately." (85) The barber went to work and, with the help of pliers, from the left side of the knight's mouth pulled a molar that was completely healthy. The clever woman took it in her hand (90) and put it carefully aside. The woman then said to the barber: "Alas, what a terrible mistake![3] (95) Have you lost your mind, having caused my dear lord so much pain that helped him little. So help me Christ, (100) you have made a big mistake, master; take a good look so that you do not fail in your art, the bad molar is on the right side of his mouth." (105) Her lord suffered great pain because he was going to be hurt twice.

The knight had to undergo more pain caused by the clever wife. The barber quickly pulled out a tooth [molar] from the right side of the mouth, from which (110) the worthy knight suffered more. A stream of blood ran over his face. The woman took the other tooth as well, being very careful with it. (115) She went quickly to the priest, to whom she gave both those molars. The priest felt very elated about things how had developed.

Now pay attention to what happened thereafter. When the priest received the teeth (120) from the woman, he went straight away to a dice maker. He brought him those two molars and insisted that he make out of them (125) two pretty, elegant small dice without delay, sparing no costs. When the dice were ready, the priest (130) went to a goldsmith without hesitation. He brought the two dice and asked him to overlay them with good silver and cast them in a socket. (135) With red gold he elegantly carved on the faces of the dice the numbers ace, deuce, trey, cater, cinque and sice, etc.[4] Those were placed well on the sides of the dice (140).

Not long afterwards, the priest happened to be in the company of the good knight, as occurs with many lovers. If he wants to love the woman, (145) he

---

[2] At first sight one could think that the narrator means "the best" when he has the knight say "der pests," but it means just the opposite, with "pests" being the superlative of the adjective "bös" or "pœse" meaning "bad," hence here "worst."

[3] Literally: "misery" or "heavy burden," but the context requires to render the word "swär" as "mistake."

[4] The narrator uses special terms for the game of dice, hence not the ordinary numbers. These are unique terms not properly translated as numbers. Here I use the words for the pips historically used for dice, borrowed directly from the French. In the original we read: "ses, zingg, drei, es, kotter, daus," which could be rendered as: "six, five, three, ace, four, three." For the history of dice, see Thomas M. Kavanagh, *Dice, Cards, Wheels*, 2005; for an excellent and detailed study online, see: http://en.wikipedia.org/wiki/Dice (last accessed on Sept. 5, 2014). See also Ulrich Vogt, *Der Würfel ist gefallen*, 2012. For the history of games and dice in the Middle Ages, see Paul Milliman, "Games and Pasttimes," *Handbook of Medieval Culture*, ed. Albrecht Classen (forthcoming).

must be on friendly terms with her husband,[5] so that he might gain the rewards of love. Thus the knight and the priest got together (150) and had a good time. The knight had no idea about the affair between the woman and the priest. The knight and the clever priest (155) played a friendly board game to have some entertainment and enjoy their friendship. But the strength of the good wine got the better of the priest and he began to chatter more (160) than was appropriate. He took the fine dice and threw them on the board. They were dice cast in silver, the faces on them (165) carved in pure red gold. The knight was very impressed and said: "I have never seen such fine and delicate dice. Neither gold nor silver were spared, (170) and they are made masterly."

The drunken priest laughed loudly and spoke with a foolish mind: "My lord, the dice themselves are not simply good because of the red gold and the fine silver. (175) They have an even greater value. The enamel of its substance has more nobility than the gold. Nor can the silver match the bone in value I assure you, (180) because the bone of these good dice used to be in the mouth of an honorable and worthy knight not long ago." When the lord heard those words, (185) he quickly understood their meaning. He kept quiet and thought about how his wife had forced him, through her evil cunning, to experience such terrible pain (190) with his teeth. He cleverly conceived a plan on how to punish both the priest and his wife physically so that they would receive (195) injuries and feel great heartfelt pain.

On the third day the knight told the priest and also his wife that he would travel to the Rhine (200) to a court in honor of a knight. He entrusted the house and his fine lady to the priest; both liked that idea. Then the knight left. (205) Soon he arranged it so that he could return home quickly in secrecy (210) and without being noticed. He went to the bedroom and hid behind a large chest without making noise. A short while afterwards, carefree, the two [lovers] opened the room. (215) The priest and the pretty wife entered together, believing that they were completely safe, but the priest was deceived, as you will soon realize. (220) A wonderful bed was readied for them, on which the priest and the delightful wife lie down. They had great fun with each other, hugging and kissing and (225) making love. They did this for a long time until night arrived and the room turned dark. The knight no longer waited (230) and silently crawled to the priest. The latter lay there, revealing that he just had made love. His balls hung down uncovered between his legs [ass cheeks]. (235) The knight grabbed the balls and the scrotum with his hands, took a knife, and cut off everything without mercy, (240) leaving nothing behind. The poor priest almost bled to death; the woman grieved greatly.

Let me leave them to their pain; (245) instead I wish to talk more about the praiseworthy knight. He left the room quickly without making noise. He had

---

[5] The original here uses the plural, but the meaning is singular.

satisfied his wish (250) to some extent, but not quite. Now, you will learn what he subsequently did. He went to his horse and left the castle (255) for well over a month until he had finished his business. He directly turned to a good tawer [leather craftsman] who was a master in his art (260) and asked him to make the scrotum into a good leather piece and to treat (lit.: dry) the balls skillfully, for which he paid him well. When all was ready, (265) the bold and valiant knight went to a leather craftswoman (lit.: merchant woman) who also made available her services. He said to her: "I beg you, (270) make a pretty bag out of the little leather piece." She carried out his charge right away. The balls were not ignored; they were attached as two buttons (275) on the bag at the top. Thereafter the lord went straight away to a goldsmith, whom he also paid (280) to beautifully decorate the two buttons and the bag with gold and silver. He paid him a good price. When he bag was finished, (285) the lord hesitated no longer and returned home.

He found his wife in mourning. She said: "My dear lord, your good friend, the priest, (290) is suffering from a great harm [sickness]. Have pity on him because he has always displayed great loyalty to you, believe me. Go and grieve with him. (295) He very much desires to see you."

The knight did not refuse and did as his wife asked him. He went to see the priest, who lay [in his bed] suffering from great pain (300) and discomfort. When the priest saw the lord, he greeted him in a friendly manner. The valiant knight thanked him for that and lamented the priest's illness, (305) but he really did not feel sorry for him. When the knight noticed that the priest complained badly, he pulled from his pocket the beautiful and precious bag. (310) He said: "I have brought you this. I think of you often and did not want to come empty-handed. This little bag is very nice and made very delicately (315) with gold and silver, by a master's hand. I want to give it to you."

When the priest saw the bag, he said: "All my suffering (320) has been eased. I will greatly enjoy this bag because it is so beautiful and valuable, which gives me new spirit." The knight replied: "However valuable it might be (325) regarding the gold and silver, the leather is much more valuable, as I will explain to you. The buttons that are attached to it and the bag itself (330) are most precious. They were recently hanging in front of a priest's ass [between the legs]. And I tell something even worse (335) than that: priest, you have no choice but to suffer bitter death right now from my own hands unless you now summon my wife (340) to you. She has always been loyal to you, and she has hugged you many times and has kissed and tongued you without end. Make her do this once more (345) or I will never forgive you. Then when she places her tongue in your mouth, you must bite it off right away without delay. (350) If you do that without hesitation, I promise you without hatred that I will not harm you and will grant you peace and penance. But if you do not do it, (355) then no one can help you and your life will end. No one will be able to prevent that."

When the priest understood those words, he was deeply frightened. (360) He wanted nothing more but that the knight would leave and let him live. He was ready to obey everything (365) the knight had asked him to do. The priest was prepared to do it so that the knight would depart.

Thereafter the miserable priest (370) immediately called for the woman, who came running to him, filled with joy. She said: "Have you gotten better?" He said: "It has never been worse. (375) But since you are here now, please extend your red lips so that my suffering will be eased." Lovingly she kissed him. He then said: (380) "Put your tongue in my mouth, my heart longs for it, I beg you my dear woman; that will ease all my pain." The woman did everything (385) he asked. She put her tongue into his mouth. The priest realized this and bit off the woman's tongue. He gave her an evil reward. (390) She lost her ability to speak. Thus was the love between those two crushed most miserably with bodily injuries and heart-felt suffering and brought to a horrible end. (395) The woman then belonged to the community of mutes. She said: "Lall lall" and nothing else. She could not say anything else and screamed: "Lall lall lall lall." She could say nothing else. (400) She ran home filled with rage. The good knight said to her: "Why do you come running home so quickly?" She answered: "Lall lall lall lall." He responded: "What has happened to you?" (405) She could not say anything else but "lall lall" all the time. He acted as if he did not know anything [about the reason] and as if he grieved for her from the bottom of his heart, but he avoided the woman from then on (410) and no longer had any dealings with her.

About half a year later the knight invited his friends to a big dinner. (415) He also invited all the friends of his wife. The knight intended to let them all know what the woman had done wrong [to him] (420) and that he would get rid of her, because she only caused him injury, shame, blame, and loss of honor, which him greatly. Although the affair had not yet become public, (425) he still suffered from it heavily.

When everyone was sitting at the table and had drunk and eaten, they all were in a great mood, as happens during festivals, (430) which create great happiness and are accompanied with many different enjoyable activities. They all chatted about pretty women and clever men (435) and related each other's adventures politely.

Finally, the husband began to tell them a funny story. He said: "Listen, old folk and young, (440) to what I have heard happened to a well-born knight. He was married to a noble lady whom he loved more than his own life. (445) But the miserable wife loved a priest more than the worthy knight and had an affair with him, since women rarely do the best thing, (450) as the ancients have already told us. The priest and the beautiful woman got together one day, as I heard it told, and had great joy with each other. (455) The priest had so much influence over her that she did whatever he wanted, because she loved him dearly [was very loyal to him]. One day the priest came up with a plan with which the wife had to comply, (460) that is, to get him two molars from the mouth of the worthy husband

without delay. The wife obeyed the priest. (465) When she came to the knight
and he wanted to hug her as before, she said that she felt very ill and turned away
from him, saying he had a rotten tooth (470) that smelled badly. She complained
much about it until he had the molar removed. Then she went one step farther
and said that it had not been the right tooth (475) convincing him to have a second tooth removed. She gave both teeth to the priest, who was very pleased with
the outcome. (480) He had two valuable dice made out of them as a mockery of
the noble knight."

Once he had finished his account, everyone present reached the same judgment: (485) that that wife deserved the penalty of losing her life. Thereupon
the worthy knight continued: "I tell you now openly that I am the same good
knight (490) from whom the teeth were pulled. But this act has not remained
unavenged, because the miserable woman has lost her tongue in payment, which
the priest bit off. (495) Also, the priest has been shit on.[6] I cleverly succeeded in
cutting off his balls. Now, you have already pronounced a judgment, saying that
the woman should lose her life (500) without being granted any mercy. I will
allow her to keep her life, and I will give her a fund of two hundred pounds or
more. (505) I want her to leave me completely and no longer live with me. The
marriage between us is dissolved, which is her own fault. I will never in my life
give her my grace [will never forgive her]."

The friends quickly took the miserable woman with them. She spoke nothing but "lall lall lall." Thus she suffered for her evil deed. With this the story has
come to an end.

---

[6] This is the literal translation. Apparently in the late Middle Ages the use of anal
language was not uncommon in the German-speaking lands, especially if we consider the
linguistic evidence in the collection of tales about *Till Eulenspiegel*, first printed in 1510,
perhaps composed by the Brunswick toll officer Hermen Bote. But the knight here oddly
mixes anal with sexual language, as the following sentence in the translation confirms.
See Albrecht Classen, *The German Volksbuch*, 1995, 185–212.

Bayertor (Bavarian Tower), Landsberg am Lech

No. 14: *The Innocent Murderess*

God never lets an innocent person be abandoned by His fatherly protection. He helps him all the time and without fail in suffering and pain. When a man is convinced (5) that he can fully rely on God and entrust Him with all his suffering, know for certain that God will never leave him behind and will always stand at his side. (10) This I want to illustrate for you with an account of how a virgin suffered much and had to bear much pain, which caused her heartfelt grief, though she was innocent and without guilt, (15) God in His grace helped her and rescued her from all her suffering.

This virgin was truly chaste, pious, pretty, and tender, and she descended from a high-ranking family. (20) She held the rank of a countess and ruled over a country. She had a good brother, a high-minded noble knight who was a true hero in his physical prowess. (25) Not far away was a king who was noble, young, and rich. He could not find a lady anywhere who held the same aristocratic rank whom he could have married (30) except for the good countess. The king began to fancy her and desired to win her as his wife. The young count immediately granted him this wish (35) and married his sister to the king, who loved her as himself. When the marriage was agreed upon, everyone said (40) that they were both equally virtuous, noble, and enjoyed the same rank. They were praised highly for their reputations.

The king had [at his court] a knight (45) who was full of rancor. He in turn had a servant who was evil and cunningly said the following words to his lord: "Listen, my dear sir, that what I tell you is true. (50) My lord the king has agreed to a bad marriage. The virgin has not been without a man until now. (55) She has had more sexual experiences than four evil women. I will arrange it in no time that she will fulfill your desire, (60) and then you will know that she is completely bad. If you follow my advice you will enjoy a great experience." When the knight heard these words (65) — he was careless and foolish — he developed evil thoughts. He said: "My dear friend, help me and give me your advice as to how I should proceed in this matter (70) in order to realize my desire. After all, the king intends to lie down with the noble maid without any delay tomorrow night and celebrate the wedding with her. (75) If I were so fortunate that I could enjoy her beforehand I would be exceedingly happy."

The servant said: "Sir, listen to me, I wish to give you good advice (80) so that you will embrace the virgin tonight, as I have planned it. Her brother, the young count, will celebrate tonight, together with his court and all his people,

(85) prenuptial festivities with his [future] brother-in-law, the noble king. They
plan to deliberate about how to carry out the wedding honorably (90) and most
effectively. At that time the maid will be alone in her strong castle. No one is
guarding her tonight except the watchman. I will ride with you to the forest
outside of the castle and stay hidden there until the early morning. (100) You
will leave your horse with me and walk on foot up to the mighty castle. Let the
guardsman know your presence and tell him in pleasant words: (105) 'Guardsman, may God reward you, tell your noble maid to let the king enter because he
wants to ask her for advice that would be good for her and him' (110). She will
not deny you this request. At dawn return to me at the spot where you left me
behind."

The knight was pleased with this suggestion. (115) They both got ready and
rode across the land toward the fortress.[1] Soon they reached a thick forest (120)
not far from the castle. At that moment they saw a large group of people approaching them on horseback, equipped with shields and lances and knightly
armor. (125) It was the noble and powerful king and his brother-in-law, the good
count. They rode happily out of the young count's castle and intended to spend
the night (130) at the king's castle; the group included all the knights and squires.

The [aforementioned] knight and his servant turned away to the side so that
no one noticed them (135) until the entire group had passed them on the road.
They did not tarry longer and turned to the splendid castle. The knight was in
good spirits (140) because he had realized that no one was in the castle who could
cause him trouble. Now the sun set and disappeared, (145) the night arrived, a
time when people like to take things that do not belong them rightfully. Whoever performs evil acts and is a thief likes the dark of night (150) and hates the
light of day.

The servant stayed quietly in the forest, keeping the two horses. The knight
secretly walked to the moat (155) and called out: "Guard, good man, tell your
noble lady that she should let me in. I am the king and stand here alone. I need
to see the chaste maid (160) to get her advice and also to tell her something that
is important for us both. If she denies me this request we both will experience
suffering without fail." (165) The guard immediately told the news to the noble
maid. She was very much frightened by these words and uncertain about what to
do. (170) "If I allow the lord to come in I will not have any power to refuse him
anything he might want which could harm my honor. [However,] I, a noble and
honorable lady, must obey him. (175) I have no choice but to live with him and
die with him because I am engaged to him. But if I do not allow him to enter,
and if he then suffers such pain (180) as he had said, he will avenge this against

---

[1] This is the literal translation; "veste" is a more archaic word, and it is used in Germany only rarely, such as for the Veste Corburg, in northern Franconia/Bavaria. We
might also use the word "stronghold," such as in the case of the Veste Oberhaus near Pas-
sau or the Veste Otzberg east of Darmstadt or straight south of Hanau.

me forever." She felt torn back and forth, deeply concerned for her own honor and worried about great damage that might affect her in the future. (185)

Finally she decided to let him in whatever might happen to her. She went to the gatekeeper and got the keys from him. (190) She asked him to accompany her quietly. He had to lower the drawbridge. The knight was admitted because he seemed to be the noble king. She led him quickly (195) to her room and said: "My dear lord, what might your business be that you have come here by yourself? I am deeply frightened." (200) He gently answered her: "Maid, believe me that I tell the truth, and I'll assure you upon my oath that I am passionately in love with you (205) and burn to be with you since you have been pledged to me as my wife. If I cannot embrace you tonight, lovely creature, my life will be wasted (210) and I will die. But if you will obey me without delay, I tell you upon my honor that I will reward you (215) forever." The maid answered: "Sir, why do you do this? I clearly understood that we will have great joy (220) tomorrow night without doubt. We will have our wedding in a very short time. I trust that you will leave me in peace (225) and wait. This is more appropriate for my honor instead of letting you fulfill your desire with me."

What can I say? He begged the maid so much (230) that she complied with his wish. She thought he was her beloved fiancé, the noble and powerful king. But he was not at all like him. He made the virgin a woman (235) when he caressed her body and spent the time full of joy with her. She also experienced much happiness and gave him much pleasure as is proper for a good woman (240) in bed with her husband. She tenderly embraced him with her white naked arms. She pressed him toward her full of love, without any cunning. (245) The knight, however, reacted to her behavior in badly. Foolishly he said: "My servant has spoken truly that the king will indeed (250) marry an evil dishonorable woman." The woman immediately asked: "What did you say?" He said: "Dear beloved wife, do not be angry with me, (255) I have become foolish as a result of my sleepiness. More I cannot say." He wished he could have taken back his words because he had spoken too much. Honestly, (260) his words hurt the beautiful lady.

After this heavy exertion the knight fell asleep. What was the woman to do? She quietly left him, (265) lit a candle, and returned with it to the man. She looked into his face and soon recognized that he was not the king. (270) She was deeply horrified that she had lost her honor in this way to this evil man. She went away filled with grief, anger, and with much agitation; (275) and looked for a strong and sharp knife, which she took with her to the bedroom. Quickly she severed the knight's head from his body, which was the pawn he had to leave behind. (280)

But now she was in trouble and went to the gatekeeper who had let the knight in. She said: "My dear friend, help me in this terrible emergency. (285) I will give you so much gold for the rest of your life that you will be rich forever. The knight who came here tonight and whom you and I admitted, (290) who called himself the king, has deceived me badly. He wanted to rob me of my honor, for which he paid with his life. I cut off his head. (295) I beg you now with all my might to help me throw the corpse into the cistern. [2] The corpse is too heavy for me. I will go with you (300) and drop the head into the well. Do not say a word about it to anyone, and I will reward you so well that you can lead a better life until your death." (305)

Quickly the gatekeeper replied: "I fully understand now that the knight has hurt you; he has slept with you. If you are willing to reward me by sharing your body with me (310), I will be ready to do what you have asked. But if you do not let me sleep with you, your begging will be for nought." The lady said: "Do not speak thus! (315) I will make you happy and raise you to a lord." He answered: "My dear lady, I will not comply with your request. I will not renounce my desire; (320) I must first have sex with you. Then I will do what I must and what you asked. If you reward me this way, it is a better payment (325) than your silver and your gold. No matter how the lady begged the servant, he would not do it, unless she allowed him to sleep with her. She was deeply grieved. (330) [3]

What can I tell you? She had no alternative and had to allow the gatekeeper to take her noble body for his sexual desires. He did with her what he lusted for, (335) just as his heart desired. After he had committed this evil deed, the lady urged the gatekeeper to go to the bedroom. He picked up the dead body (340) and heaved it on his shoulder. The lady carried the head. Then both went to the cistern. She could not forbear this, and said to the gatekeeper: (345) "Now, bend over carefully and let the corpse drop into the water without making any noise so the watchman does not hear the splash." (350) The gatekeeper followed her order, bent over with the corpse so that he could let it fall into the cistern silently. (355) The lady was clever and smart and [immediately] lifted him up by his feet and threw him into the water, this traitor of a gatekeeper—bravo! [4] This was his reward for [ill-conceived] love. (360) He immediately drowned at the bottom of the water. She threw down the [severed] head herself.

She did not tarry there (365) and quickly returned to her chamber. The bed linens were stained red with blood. She was deeply worried about how to clean it all up so that no one would notice anything. (370) She washed and worked hard and did not find any rest until dawn. She made every effort until she arranged all so that no one could learn anything (375) about this event.

Now, as the day broke, the [evil knight's] servant waited in the forest not far from the castle. He strained to see when his lord (380) would return from the castle and come back to him as they had agreed upon. He worried about his lord. He waited on the meadow almost until noon, (385) when the young count came

---

[2] "Cistern" is the better word choice by Simmons, which I happily copy. It complies directly with the original term used by the narrator, "cistern."

[3] Simmons uses the odd translation: "For that reason she had to be sad."

[4] The narrator explicitly voices this opinion, supporting the lady's action in this terrible situation.

home riding through the forest, fully armored, together with his entourage. He wanted to get to his castle quickly and to his chaste sister. (390) When they came closer and discovered the servant who held a stallion [knightly horse] in hand they rushed up to him and questioned him (395) regarding his business there. Fearfully he tried to avoid them. He was neither smart nor intelligent in this situation because he harbored no good intentions. They charged him with being evil and vile (400) and openly accused him of having stolen the two horses. They beat him gravely, and then they hung him from a tree branch for everyone to see. (405) He choked so much that he soon died. He had earned his death because he had given evil advice that led to both the knight's (410) and the gatekeeper's death. Moreover, the maid had been placed in a dire situation at his suggestion. She lost the greatest honor that God had granted her. (415) This was the result of the evil advice that this scoundrel had given. Let him hang there.

The count cheerfully arrived in his mighty castle (420) and told his sister about this event. She mulled it over it but said nothing because she well understood the connection between these events. Then the count said: (425) "Sister, prepare yourself now without delay. We must go to the wedding. The king will marry and has chosen you as his wife. (430) Today you will be his bride. Be ready, my sister." She was frightened because she had lost her honor [virginity] by being cheated by a malicious man. (435) Nevertheless the sorrowful and unhappy lady prepared herself immediately, together with all her maids, as did the count with his entourage. The maid was brought to the king (440) at court with all expected honors. The noble king was very happy about it and welcomed her respectfully and in a friendly manner. The young woman, however, sat there feeling deep pain. Whereas everyone else was filled with happiness, (445) the lady lamented bitterly and secretly in her heart. She suffered deeply in her sorrow and prayed to mighty God. Although she had much sadness in her heart, (450) her behavior revealed nothing of her distress.

Then the dinner was ready. The king and the pretty lady, the count and many noble knights, (455) and also many beautiful women sat at the table. They were served large quantities of venison and fish, and whatever else was appropriate for such a feast. (460) They lived well and had enough food. [Nevertheless,] much was left over and then carried away. After they had eaten plentifully and the tables had been cleared, (465) many musicians with trumpets and pipes played for their entertainment and sang many songs.[5]

Afterwards the king went to bed. The count took his sister (470) and led her, holding her with both his arms, to the chamber. When she got to the bed, she quickly turned to one of her maids (475) whom she trusted most. She said: "Send everyone away!" This was done immediately. The lady, her maid, and the noble

---

[5] Literally, the narrator refers to "trombones," but in the context of his time, "trumpets" is the correct term. The original here is in the passive voice (as Simmons has it as well), but the active voice seems to work better.

king (480) remained there alone; all the others were told to leave. The king lay down on the bed. The maid took care of the light. The queen said to her: (485) "Accompany me to the outside, I need to use the bathroom."[6] They did so immediately. They both left the room with the light. (490) The queen said politely: "Listen to what I ask from you. I trust you especially, please be grateful in return. When we return to the room, (495) to the king, my lord, quench the light immediately and be mindful of all the good things I have ever done for you. Lie down in the bed (500) next to my dear lord and remain until he has satisfied his desires with you. I promise to give you as reward endless amounts (505) of gold and silver upon my oath, enough to fill your chests, but swear to me in return that you will leave the bed right away (510) when I ask you tonight."

The maid did not object and swore to the queen without guile (515) to do everything she had asked. Then they entered the chamber and put out the light. The maid did not hesitate (520) and lay down with the king without saying a word, just as if she were the queen. The queen stood nearby and heard what happened. (525) The king embraced the maid and made love to her as he desired. He held her tightly to himself and made that virgin a woman. (530) The queen heard everything because she was not far away, standing quietly in the chamber.

When the king had satisfied his desire with the maid, (535) the queen became nervous. She waited restlessly until the king had fallen asleep and began to snore. Then she hesitated no longer (540) and approached the bed. She asked the maid to leave the bed as she had promised to do. But the maid did not want to do it (545) and was not agreeable nor spoke to her in a friendly manner. The queen became deeply frightened. Once again she begged the maid (550) not to behave so badly and to stay steadfastly loyal as she had promised. But no matter what the queen begged or said, it did not help.(555) The maid did not want to leave; she wanted to be queen herself, which was a great problem for the [real] queen and dire trouble. She never experienced greater sorrow. (560) She paced the chamber and would have almost lost her mind. Then she decided to try (565) once again, returned to the bed as before, and begged the maid even more not to commit such a crime against her. The maid's shouts in response (570) resounded in the entire chamber. She spoke with a piercing voice, disregarding the danger that the king might wake up. But he was so deeply asleep that he heard nothing (575) of their quarrel.

The queen had to abandon the idea of being with the king, though she would have loved to lie with him. She no longer dared ask [the maid] to let herself be with the king. (580) Many thoughts crossed her mind. As she stood there heavy with sadness and a grievous heart, she heard that the maid had also fallen asleep. (585) She carefully thought by herself how to cause pain to the maid as well. She secretly went to the kitchen and lit a torch without making any noise (590)

---

[6] Simmons translates correctly and literally: "to see to my comfort," but the situation here leaves no choice but to render this as "use the bathroom."

She returned to the chamber with it and set fire in all four corners, making the chamber go up in flames. Then she rushed to the bed where the king lay asleep. (595) She took off her dress and stood there stark naked. She embraced the king and pulled him off the bed. She shouted: "Get up, my dear husband! (600) We must escape from here if we do not want to die in this house from the fire, which is burning hard and fierce." The king jumped up immediately (605) and thanked his wife because she had rescued him from danger. They barely managed to run through the door out of the chamber.[7] The queen locked it with the bolt (610) and left with the king. The maid in the chamber burned to fine ash. Losing her life was the proper reward (615) for her great disloyalty.

The king and the noble lady loved each other and lived well together. She was very loyal the noble king, (620) her lord. He was equally loyal to her, this noble and beautiful lady. After they had lived together for thirty-two years in this way, (625) as I have been told, the noble king rested one day with his head in her lap asleep. The lady mused about many things (630) and was rueful for having taken the knight's life; and she felt sorry for him, and for having killed the gatekeeper and the maid, because that the disloyal servant (635) also had to die. This all returned to her mind and she began to cry so hard that the tears dropped onto the king's face. He [woke up] and said: "My dear wife, (640) tell me what has happened to you? Indeed, I have never seen you filled with so much sadness. Let me know, good woman, who has done harm to you! (645) He will have to pay for it with his life." The lady could not hold back. She was filled with so much grief that her husband decided to get to the bottom of her problem and solve it. (650) But he had to promise her not to be wrathful or angry. This he pledged to her.

The lady began to tell him (655) how the noble knight had come to her at night cunningly pretending to be the king, then had slept with her, and finally betrayed himself (660) through the words that he had spoken to her, for which he had to give his head in payment. Then she told the king how she had been raped [forced] by the gatekeeper who caused her much misery, (665) and how she then had thrown him into the deep cistern. Moreover, she revealed to the king how the guardian outside of the castle [the servant], who had been the cause of the crime committed against her (670) by giving evil advice that had robbed her of her honor, had been hanged from a tree. Finally, she related to the king how she had talked with the maid (675) who had lain with the king on the first wedding night in her place. Because she had pleaded with this "fine" maid to leave the bed to no avail,[8] (680) the latter had to die a miserable death through the painful fire that she, the queen, had set herself. (685) All this she revealed to her husband.

Once she finished her account, the king tenderly embraced his wife and pulled her toward him, full of love: "You had to pay dearly for me," (690) he said

---

[7] Simmons ignored this adverbial expression, "gar genot," which, however, strongly heightens the dramatic situation here, hence needs to be translated as well.

[8] Simmons ignores this adjective, which specifically intensifies the ironic element here.

to the lady. "I want to live with you forever as your loyal servant because you have suffered much on my behalf, no doubt about it. (695) Neither your honor nor my appreciation of you will ever be diminished through any punishment, either secretly or publicly, because of this story." This was the good man's pledge upon his honor (700) to the lady.

In my opinion the noble king acted properly because the lady never did anything evil and yet fell into great sorrow (705) without guilt or intention [on her part]. But those who had stolen her honor paid dearly for it because each of them had to pawn his life. (710) It was only justice what happened to the knight's servant because of his evil counsel: He was hanged like an ordinary thief. He gave an advice to his lord that was wrong and based on a lie. (715) For this he was hanged on a branch. The knight also had to suffer his penalty because of the extremely evil deed he committed against the queen, when he deceived her with his words (720) and robbed her of her honor [virginity]. For this reason she cut the head off his beautiful body.[9] The gatekeeper received his proper punishment from the queen (725) and so lost his life when he drowned in the cistern, after he had abused her noble body against her own will, forcing her to sleep with him.[10] (730) What happened to the maid when she burned to ashes in the fire was also just because she had wanted to have the king as her husband and stay with him forever. (735) For this she received harsh payment, which pleases me because she was full of disloyalty. All of them suffered the right penalty.

I would be happy (740) if the same befell everyone of whom one knows without a doubt that they lead a life of evil and dishonesty. (745) Truly, I am pleased; it seems good and proper when disloyalty strikes its own author, as happened to those four people. Nevertheless, the lady, so free of any cunning (750)—I mean the queen—had to suffer great misery. Because she had no evil [intent] in her, instead only goodness, (755) God granted her His mercy. He rescued her from all dangers. She would have died from her suffering if God had not assisted her repeatedly. He does so to all (760) who fall into danger from no fault of their own.

Herewith the tale comes to its conclusion, told to you by Kaufringer.

---

[9] While "bottich" normally means "barrel," "vat," or any other large wooden container, in some contexts it can also refer to the human body, as in this case, according to the *Deutsches Rechtswörterbuch* (http://drw-www.adw.uni-heidelberg.de/drw-cgi/zeige?index=1 emmata&term=bottich; last accessed on Sept. 5, 2014).

[10] Literally: "to be his wife."

City wall in Polcenigo, north of Pordenone, west of Udine, Italy

No. 15: *The Fur-Lined Blanket*

I no longer want to keep quiet, I have to tell you a story about a beautiful and clever woman who carried out a plan in a smart way (5) to deceive her husband who was, to tell the truth, blind with his eyes open. Many women can manipulate a simple-minded man (10) with all sorts of tricks so that he will swear a hundred oaths that he was not cuckolded by her. She pulls the wool over his eyes with clever words (15) so that he is her fool, as the woman about whom I tell this adventure did to her husband. Now listen to what happened. (20)

The woman of whom I am telling about here had the habit of always resting at noon time in her room to take a nap (25). One day she called in her lover, who soon came to lie down on the bed with his pretty lady after taking off his clothes. They exchanged pleasantries (30) because they were in love with each other. They played the game of love in a delightful way. Soon thereafter the husband happened to enter the room. (35) The woman immediately grabbed a blanket, which she wrapped around herself. She got up from the bed. She carefully thought about what to do and how she could (40) deceive her husband. She said: "Come here to me and tell me the truth. Would you like it or hate it if another man were lying here with me (45) in bed, looking for my womanly love and wanting to enjoy my body?" Those were the words of the clever woman. "What would you do about that? Would I then have peace (50) from you or punishment?" The man understood very little of what the woman meant with these words. He answered: "Truly, I think, he [the lover] would suffer my wrath. (55) Judging from your words [however], I assume that you want to poke fun at me." In response the woman said: "But tell me after all what you would do, (60) if a man were lying here with me, or shall I tell you how I would handle the situation?"

Naively the good man responded: "I would like to learn that from you." (65) Immediately she pulled her husband over to her. She grabbed his head and wrapped the blanket around it. She pressed him to her chest so strongly (70) that he neither heard nor saw anything. She said to her husband: "I would act in this way. I would say without hesitation: 'He who has his clothing on (75) shall not depart from me. He who is naked should quickly take his leave! Indeed, I will not let go of my dear husband, whom I hold tightly." (80) She pressed him hard against her for a long time until the worthy guest had walked through the door with no problem. [Only] then did she let her husband go without struggling with him further. (85) But he could hardly [if at all] understand what had really occurred. He said, without suspecting anything: "You have numbed me and pressed my head really hard. (90) Really, it is no fun if you joke with me without cause." Immediately she lovingly offered him her red lips. (95) Thus all worked out just fine [between them], and the lover escaped without trouble. Thus our story has come to an end.

No. 16: *The Three Temptations of the Devil*

By my oath I advise you, since the devil is filled with great hatred against the entire world, that both high- and low-ranking people ought to guard against sin and evil deeds. (5) The devil pursues us with such open enmity toward humanity that he thinks constantly about how to make people act against God's grace. (10) He bets on it; he cares neither for clothing nor for food, neither for this nor for that, but only of how he might catch us in sins ever more frequently and grave (15) so that we have to enter hell. He is filled with so much envy and hatred of us only for that reason. If we ever become his companions in the eternal torture of hell, (20) we would suffer a hundred times more pain than ever before. With evil and silent practices he gives advice and inspires people (25) to give in to sinfulness. No one sees or hears anything when the hellish throng misleads people through words or images. He allows sin to remain in existence (30) so that it always stays in force. Thus the body is built by the false devil's advice. But he has no power over the soul, rest assured. (35) After all, if the army of evil devils had power over the soul, they would not allow anyone to survive here. God alone has power over the soul. He has granted us through His pure grace (40) both senses and a mind so that we can differentiate between evil and good, so that we can resist the devil's advice and bad influence, so that we may well survive the strike of eternal damnation, (45) which no one can resist. I mean the horrible pain of hell, which no one can get used to. If someone might stay there for hundred thousand years, (50) the torture still hurts as much as on the first day. Hence we must have a good [clear?] mind and reject the devil's temptation, must flee from deadly sin, (55) and turn toward virtues. We really are in need of that.

To tell the truth, three dangerous traps are set for holy Christendom (60) by the trickery of devils. No one is so poor, so rich, so young, so old, holds so much power, or is so learned or so wise (65) that [devils] do not still secretly ambush him in every possible manner and use great lies, both day and night, because that is all that concerns them, how they might lead us (70) into the eternal sorrow of hell. The truth of that is demonstrated by the Book of Judges, where you can read: There is a great city called Gaba, (75) where people felt really terrible fear. It was besieged by a large army. The hostile soldiers placed themselves silently around that city so that no one could see them. Quietly they were on guard, (80) watching how they could hurt all the people, both poor and rich who lived in that city, both physically and materially because they harbored great hatred against them. (85) They had all sworn that those whom they would be able to capture would have to lose their lives. The people of the city came riding out, boldly and fearlessly (90) and fought against the enemy. Then they returned without having suffered any damage. Those who remained in the city (95) did not want to spare themselves any longer because they had been successful before. The gates were opened and they rode out, attacking the enemies again. Then they returned home without having suffered anything, (100) filled with great joy. They no longer hesitated and wanted to cause their enemies (105) great unrest [exert pressure] without offering peace and the chance for penance, wishing to ruin them all. The citizens made great noise and were filled with happiness because they had succeeded twice. (110) They quickly rode out of the city again, aggressively without fear and wanting to hunt for honor again. They were twelve thousand men or more. Yet all were slain (115) by those who camped outside of the city. They were trapped so badly that only six hundred men escaped back into the city. All the others were slain. (120) Saint Paul, the holy servant of God, was born of the family descending from one of them.

You have to understand from this the three traps and lies that devils set for us deceptively here in this world [at this time]. (125) They are so filled with envy yet never successful in winning the city. They feel their hatred a hundred-fold more against us, if they carefully consider (130) how to catch us and give us everlasting death. Every good Christian ought to know about the first ambush that the devils have prepared (135) for poor Christendom. That happens, as I have heard, as soon as we are born and begin to live here on earth [original sin]. I am going to tell you of the second ambush: (140) that is, when we traverse the world. I will not leave out the third ambush, which also needs to be noted: when we depart from this world.

Now, let me explain (145) the first ambush that I mentioned. It happens when we step into this world and the miserable devils have trapped us, as I said (150). The first ambush [sin] begins before baptism. The devils all speculate that the child will die without having been baptized, because they well know that then it will never encounter God's face. (155) Humans lost that chance beforehand through their arrogance. Sometimes a woman is afraid of the evil-minded world when she delivers a child (160) [probably in the meaning: out of wedlock]. Then the devil seduces her to grant the child no peace and to take its life. That way she would preserve her honor. I mean hereby those daughters [women] (165) who are not married. Unfortunately it often happens through them that they follow the false advice of the hate-filled devil so that they remove their new born (170) from Christian baptism and kill their own blood. The devil also does not refrain from trying hard to tell an ignorant mother how to behave before the child is born. (175) He often advises the foolish woman to go jumping, dancing, or hopping, and to step or jump carelessly, (180) or he makes her lean over a chest. Or he makes the husband, in a terrible wrath, abuse the wife and beat her. All this is brought about by the miserable devil when he tries to ruin the child. (185)

When the right time and moment have come for the child to be born, then the devil turns all his attention to planning how to destroy the child so that it dies without holy baptism. (190) He sometimes advises that people wait for baptism until there are enough godparents on hand. Then if one is missing whom one would have liked to be a godparent, (195) how quickly the devil causes one to wait two or three days, so that the baptism is postponed even more, because the child might die in the meantime. When the priest arrives (200) for the baptism then, you can observe that he works hard, as he should and as is customary, so that he causes trouble for the devil by not further delaying the baptism. (205) Nevertheless, the devil exerts his influence. When the people are in the process of baptizing, he causes someone still to get confused and not say the right words so that the baptism becomes invalid. (210) An improper baptism is also the first ambush and deception that the devil makes.

The second ambush comes after the baptism, (215) as I will explain to you. As soon as the child is baptized, the devils send one of them right away to always stay the child, to advise it and teach it (220) to cry and whimper all the time, all of which trigger unclean cuss words and curses to which the child thus becomes accustomed from early on. When the child displays such evil behavior and knows how to act thusly (225) already in its early years, both father and mother are happy that it possesses such intelligence and leans toward evil behavior. The devil thus reveals his teaching, (230) when the child assumes a habit that it can hardly ever dismiss and will never let go of evilness. What one acquires in the youth as a habit stays with the person until the old age (235) and can hardly be overcome. Both father and mother ought to avoid that and should raise the child in every respect to pursue honor and virtue. It should be very painful for (240) people to hear a bad word from the mouth of their child. One should punish a little child with a small rod that does not hurt badly. (245) One ought to drive out evil and terrible habits that a child has received from the devil. But it is a common phenomenon that father and mother happily laugh (250) when a child acts like a rascal. But that is not good in any sense because the child thus acquires an evil attitude.

Because a child hardly ever gets rid of this behavior (255) when it grows up, becoming more impudent from day to day, God will not let his father and mother go unpunished; they will have to suffer pain [in turn] (260) and do penance for the child. If they had not allowed it to develop its own will, they would have raised the child in virtue and piety (265). [Since they did not do it], they will face pain and be struck just as an abbot is punished for the members of his monastery, as is a bishop for his priests, (270) and the priest for his parishioners. One ought to teach a child the *Pater Noster* and the [right] faith and turn it away from being a rascal to a virtuous person, and then it will get used to doing good deeds (275) and not be hurt by the devil's ambush.

Now as we all become adults, as I tell you, having gone through the first ambush and deception, we are placed on the scale. (280) When we traverse the world, it becomes necessary for us to protect ourselves properly from the second ambush that the evil hellish servants set up secretly, (285) covered by two types of lies. The first lie is unjustified fear; the other one, as you can read, is illicit love, as I will tell you. All sins result from these two. (290) Many sins are the result of the first sin, as I am teaching you. Through this the devils quickly gain power over countless people. Many people commit deadly sins (295) by fearing worldly authorities much more than God. One person might fear public mockery, another fears poverty, a third fears threats. For example, a lord tells his farmhand (300) to commit what is called a deadly sin. The farmhand immediately follows that command out of fear so that the lord does not hate him. Similarly, when a wife often fears her husband (305) and then does something because he forces her, although it is inappropriate and evil, that is a wrong kind of fear and is done against God. (310)

One encounters many intelligent men who can give good counsel, but who rather prefer to abandon the right path [law] than to lose popularity among the people, and that is against God. (315) I tell you this without kidding: every wise person should rather lose life and goods than to commit any kind of deadly sin, (320) because it is certainly better to lose life and material goods than for the devils to fetter you and take you down to hell. The disloyal dogs of hell (325) wanted to trap Saint Peter through this deception when he was filled with wrong fear and denied any knowledge of Christ. But repentance helped him again, (330) so that he was saved.

The other deception contrived in an evil manner, which the traitor devil does to us impudently in the second ambush, is called illicit love. (335) I will tell you about this lie. It consists of three types, as you can read. The first is love of the flesh. The second is wrong love of honor. The entire world turns to the third type, (340) which is love for illicit goods, through which countless poor souls are lost.

As I have mentioned before, (345) the love of the flesh is a gate that leads to hellish fire. Through that lie and ambush the devils almost took away, to their profit, King David, (350) except that he then felt great remorse. He escaped the useless power of the devil and so remained uninjured. King Solomon, who was endowed with more wisdom (355) than all other people, nevertheless became a victim of that sin, the illicit love of miserable flesh, and so he committed a deadly sin. Whether or not he paid penance for it (360) I do not want to discuss here.

The Bible also informs us that lust for the flesh caused Samson, the strong man, to lose all his strength (365) when a woman shaved off his hair, in which his strength rested. Therefore, keep yourself on guard both night and day so that you will not be nourished (370) by wrong and evil love. I mean [love of] the flesh and the bodily organs through which many souls are caught and have become prisoners [children] of hell. Do not look for happiness (375) by pursuing the pleasures of the flesh. Do not allow the flesh to control you and don't submit in any way to gluttony. You will not be denied what you need (380) in terms of food or drink. Also, your heart should not desire to break the marriage vow, because that sin weakens you. These are actual causes of sinfulness, the pursuance of the wrong love of the flesh. (385) The throng of disloyal devils pushes you to do it so that you become their slaves [relatives].

Wrong love is the other ambush; I mean the wrong love of honor. Whosoever believes that he (390) might thus attract many friends and companions through words and other things so that they honor him will quickly realize (395) that he will never find good counsel. You devil, you have abducted many people through an ambush who must now face eternal pain. But women are lured most to sin (400) by evil vanity. A woman places a curly headgear that has more than twenty points with which she tries to elevate herself so that people praise her (405) wherever she might display it proudly. But it turns out to be nothing but a little cloth with yellow tips woven into it. Believe me, without offense, she pleases none by it (410) except the devil, for sure. [Women], you are going to lose access to the heavenly kingdom just because of this little form of vanity, believe me on my honor.[1]

The third deception of the ambush (415) consists of evil love for goods. That is a horrible deception, indeed. Everyone is full of inappropriate desire for material things. One person satisfies it through theft, (420) another through robbery, the next through grabbing, the next through all kinds of thievery, and thus they gain their goods against God's will. One person practices his art in a dangerous manner (425) and thus becomes rich in material terms; another does it through deception, another through salesmanship, and another through yet a different strategy. One person takes up usury; for another the best way is to pawn (430) part of his land without providing any surety based on his whole estate. These are all wrong methods, and thereby people like false and evil goods more than God. (435) That is against the First Commandment because we should love God with all our strength in all regards.

Generally the whole world's love for material things and money is wrong. (440) People are misled by the devil's evil strategy, which is part of the deception. The false and cursed devil tempted God Himself. When Christ was on a mountain, (445) the devil conceived the idea: "He is always anxious to bring together a whole throng of souls from all over the world. I will promise him some goods (450) and he will quickly consider: 'I will gain many souls therewith.'" He wanted to deceive God [thereby]. In his evil mind the devil said to God: "See there all those countries! (455) They all belong to me. I will turn them all over to you, if you bow before me [submit yourself] and worship me, I kid you not, as your lord and god." (460) Thereupon our Lord Christ said right away to the devil; "Go away, you evil Satan! You are empty of all virtues. No one may pray to you. (465) How dare you embrace the illusion that you could tempt your Lord? One must worship my Father."

---

[1] Here, as at many other times, the narrator refers to "his loyalty" when uttering an oath that he is telling the truth. It might be more idiomatic to say "honor" in such cases.

Now, I am afraid that nowadays, since there is great love for money, (470) many miserly people will be led away through this ambush. The person who despairs in God would rather take the road to hell than to let go wrongly acquired wealth (475) and thus will abandon God's grace and also His mercy. Oh, you throng of devils, you never give up your assault of those who by night and by day (480) engage their mind and thought only on how to gain material wealth, in opposition to God and honor. They will therefore have to sit ever more, just because of small and contemptible goods, (485) in the hellish fire [glow]. I mean both them and all their children, and those who inherit those goods knowing about their origin.

Now, I have interpreted the two types of traps that the devil (490) sets up for us, as you have heard. The first one happens right after we have been born, the other happens when we live here in this world. (495) If we can protect ourselves from both without suffering anything at the hand of the devils, they are still on the lookout quietly. They have arranged yet the third ambush, (500) which is very dangerous. May the benevolent God protect us from it! This happens when we are losing our life (505) and are about to die, ready to depart from this world. It will be necessary for us to be protected from them particularly at that moment.

They have, these envious cursed devils, created two traps out of envy. (510) They tempted God Himself in that ambush, these servants from hell, trying to capture Him. Our Lord knew that well. (515) That night when he was ready to suffer the pain of death He spoke with sorrow to his dear disciples: "The prince of hell will arrive tomorrow for sure, as I tell you. (520) He intends to tempt me, but he will not succeed because he will not find any [weakness] in me." The devil came, as was his ardent desire, on the morning of Good Friday (525) to God Himself, who was attached [lied on] to the cross of branches, where the Divinity was loaded [covered] with the many sins of mankind, and he tried to determine whether he might capture (530) the soul at that moment. Since the situation was such that God could not be spared, He had to be tempted during the pain of death by the devil. (535) How then should we poor people here on earth ever have peace and protection, and what should we do during the hour of our death that we will not be misled by the devil?

The devils in their cleverness (540) assume that they might steal from us two virtues that we have received from God. They torture their minds how to gain them from us when we are in the throes of death. (545) May God then protect us so that we can escape all their ambushes. You Christians must understand what the first pure virtue is: that is the Christian faith by itself, (550) which the devils like to steal from us when we depart from this world. Oh, all you ignorant devils, how much you like to take away from people during the last breath (555) the pure virtue, noble and fine, that is the Christian faith. You [devils] do that with intention: you all well know, you hellish Moors, that you have lost all your honor (560) because of the pure Christian faith. During the time of the Old Law [the Old Testament] people brought you sacrifices and paid you great respect. All that was nothing in the face of God. (565) The Christian faith has put you to shame and deprived you of all your honor.

If a person wants to be perfect in the Christian faith, living the proper life (570) without being counted among the unfaithful people, he must be firm in his faith. A person who wonders in his or her mind and is filled with doubt (575) about which the right faith might be, whether the Jews, the heretics, or the pagans are correct, and does not know what the truth is, has already been kidnapped (580) by the devilish crowd through their cunning, and is thus brought away from the proper faith.

You must be firm in your faith, like stone selected for the foundation [of a house]; strong and good. (585) The person who has courage to erect such a house will build one that will stand and last for a long time against winds and the force of rain. The person who builds a house on sand creates one without good stability (590) because the foundation is so weak that rain and the force of wind undermine it so that it will collapse quickly. By the foundation built on sand (595) you can recognize the faith of heretics. The wind is the devil's cunning, and the rain storm is the Antichrist.

Therefore, all you Christians, if you love heaven (600) never veer from the faith. When the heretics come crawling to you with their wrong faith, the foundation will be built badly on sand without a good [great] harbor. (605) Do not allow them to undermine your building; do not follow them and remain steadfast. When the wind blows at you and tears at you fiercely (I mean thereby the devilish creatures from hell), (610) then remain steadfast and strong. When the Antichrist arrives at last like a forceful thunderstorm, then the foundation of your house ought to be built in such a way, well firmed and protected (615), that you would rather lose life and goods at his hands than fall away from the right faith. If then your father and mother came down (620) from the other world and tried to convince you to turn away from your faith, do not follow their teaching.

You must solidify the foundation before death so that it does not break at the end in this way. (625) Every person ought to confess his faith ardently, without interruption, at least twice a day, that is, in the morning when you get up and in the evening when you go to sleep. (630) The purpose of this is to confirm your faith all the time without any detraction.[2] Believe me, this hymn is neither false nor a deception. It was invented a long time ago (635) and begins thus: "Now we beg the Holy Ghost for the right faith above all so that it protects us until our death when we leave this miserable life." (640) You ought to sing it every day with a loud voice and full of devotion so that the devil cannot rob you at the end of the right faith.

---

[2] The entire syntactical structure implies a conditional clause that is not followed through by the narrator; instead he is content with simple affirmative statements about the value of the right faith. This forced me to restructure the entire section, making it an affirmative sentence.

Now, you may observe a custom (645) that there is in our time in some monasteries that when someone approaches death, then all who live in that community congregate (650) and recite the Pater Noster [faith] so that the devil cannot
pull him from the path of the right faith. And this is the truth: "Follow the right
faith (655), death will thus weaken the devil since he cannot cause him any harm.
He will have peace and protection from him."

The other virtue that we possess and which the evil servants of hell (660)
want to rob us of when we turn away from this world is hope. After all, Judas,
who despaired, (665) was caught in that very ambush and deception because
he did not have the virtue of hope, since the devils had robbed him of it. If he
had repented, accepted his penance, and had embraced hope, God would have
blessed him (670) by allowing him to regain grace. All his evil deeds and guilt
would have been forgiven, just as Saint Peter was; be assured of that. But the
devils blew at him (675) and did not grant him any respite, when he had betrayed
Christ. They cleverly told him: "Oh dear, what have you done! What will happen
with you?" (680)

They filled him with so much fear that he completely lost the virtue that is
called hope. They planted doubt in him so that he despaired of God. (685) His
dull mind drove him to rage and to rave: "I have sold innocent blood," said the
cursed man. He then searched for a rope (690) and hanged himself. Thus the
devils begin every day without fail, when we are approaching death, and cleverly
consider (695) how they might take away at that moment this virtue, which is
called firm hope. Whenever we suffer from worries and fear at the moment of
death, (700) the false devilish throng adds other faults and feelings of guilt. They
have written it all down, have not forgotten or left out anything, be sure of that.
(705) They bring everything together and pile it in a big heap and make the feelings of horror great and the evil deeds huge. When a person lets go of hope (710)
and no [longer] leaves aside his doubts, he will be lost forever.

Now let me give you an advice so that hope does not abandon you in the last
moment of your life (715) and that you shed all doubt. You must be firm every
day until your end, while you live, in serving God both early in the morning and
late in the evening. Practice repentance and do your confession (720) on a daily
basis, based on complete repentance. Do not be lame in practicing virtues: give
alms, pray, and fast. That will make the pile of sin and unclean deeds thin and
small (725), and increases the pile of good deeds. When the time comes to depart
from here and you approach death, and when then the devils bring many charges
(730) concerning your guilt and misdeeds, then the angels come together and argue against the devils' lying and place the good deeds on the scale.

When a person then notices (735) that the angels bring many virtues [that
he had practiced in life] to help him, such as alms, prayer, and fasting, and that
the pile of good deeds is growing thereby, (740) then a man will be very pleased.
Doubt will dwindle thereby. Even if the pile of evil deeds would be great and

Bridge crossing a canal in Bruges, Belgium, leading to the town center

heavy and outweigh the good deeds, (745) still the brave person should remain steadfast without doubt and have good hope for God and His graces.

On my honor, I tell you, (750) if a person has a strong mind, God will place His torture [that He had suffered] and His blood in the middle of the pile and thus outweigh altogether the evil deeds placed there by devil, (755) who raises charges against man without mercy. God has freed us strongly, so He may protect us all the time, as long as we turn away from sin. (760) Thus, while God grants him life, everyone ought to, live in virtue both early and late, since the devil does not let anyone be free of temptation, causing damage. (765) Saint Martin was not exempt from this temptation when approaching death. The devil also lied to him at the last turn of his life. (770) He said to the devil: "You bloody creature, you really will not find anything in me; everything has been repented."

Now each of you must greet Mary (775) with an "Ave Maria," so that she, a pure virgin, will help gain for all Christendom in the name of her son Jesus Christ, who is the lord of all creatures (780) and who cannot deny any of her requests, protection from the devil's lies at all times as we traverse this world and then pass from this life. (785) We beg that the cunning and plans of devils, wherever they might be positioned to aim at us, will ultimately fail despite all their lies. (790) We hope that their strategies will not hurt our body and our soul. Thus says Heinrich Kaufringer.

No. 17: *The Pious Miller's Wife*

Some time ago there was a miller's wife about whom much was written that she commanded [many] virtues. She loved God with all her might in her pure heart, without doubt. (5) Two priests, who both belonged to the Order of the Franciscans [Order of the Preachers, or Friars], learned about her, namely that this woman loved God from the bottom of her heart and could speak sweetly about God. (10)

These two men decided to pay her a visit in order to meet that pure woman. They both agreed to find this woman right away (15) to gain some divine teaching.

It happened that they soon found the poor house of a miller. It was the one where the woman lived for whom they had steadfastly looked. (20) In front of the house two children were sitting. The two men went directly to the house without making much noise. Each one of the children had, in their childish manner, built a little house. (25) One of them spoke to the other in a friendly manner: "Now you have to say a Pater Noster, since my house is much stronger than yours." (30) The other child replied: "In fact, you do me injustice with your words and threat, so you have to pay with an Ave Maria, since my house is stronger than yours." (35) To this the other child responded intelligently and in a polite manner: "Well, you think that you are attractive and smart and not lacking in wisdom. What would you prefer: (40) that God the Lord rests in you, or would it be your desire that you yourself rested in God?" The other child immediately answered seriously and said: "Oh God, what are you asking me (45) with your foolish words! If God were in me, the highest treasure, I would soon lose Him if I used arrogant words. Why would it not be the better choice (50) that I would be in God, my Lord? Then it would be difficult [impossible] for Him to abandon me. I would never lose him."[1]

Then the other child said in response: (55) "Are you still fasting? Let me know." The other answered with a good conscience: "No, I have eaten something." The other: "What have you eaten? Let me know." (60) He said: "I will tell you. I have seen in the priest's hand the holy Host of Jesus Christ, which is food for the soul, taking us to the eternal life. (65) It completely feeds my soul, as bread does for the body against the bitter suffering of hunger."

---

[1] This is, indeed, a heavy theological debate, here placed in the children's mouths, in order to emphasize their mother's religiosity and virtues, since she raised those children.

The two priests were standing next to them and listened to the children's words. (70) They said to each other: "If these are the branches [children], how perfect then might be the trunk [mother]." They approached the children and asked them where their mother was. (75) The children told them without hesitation: "She is sitting and doing her prayer and says the Pater Noster, since she carries out her daily prayers and has thus not gotten to her daily bread. (80) Once she has eaten her breakfast, she will come out and give us right away our breakfast without us asking for it. Then our mother returns (85) to her prayer."[2]

The two men then went to the house where they found the miller's wife, the pure woman, kneeling and saying her prayer all by herself. (90) They both greeted her openly and said: "Dear sister, tell us, your house is situated here in the forest far from the church and the people. (95) When will the priest interpret God's words for you, or when have you heard a sermon, or when have you made a confession?" She answered: "Lords, this year I have heard (100) only one sermon, indeed, by my lord, the priest. I still keep it completely in my heart, be assured of that. I have taken from it every day (105) some teaching, I assure you. So far I still have barely reflected on [and understood] the meaning and blessing of half of those words. Tell me, when I confess, (110) is it better to lie about a sin than to go to confession every day? Let me tell you as a fact that my husband, the miller, and the bag in the mill (115) that I often have to carry back and forth, detract me [in my effort] to live a divine life."

The lords sat down with her and joined with her (120) in divine love and delight and questioned the miller's wife first of all what the beginning of a divine life would be like. She said: "I will tell you that. (125) When you discover a person displaying patient humbleness who is yet burdened by poverty the she or he willingly accepts, who also loves God from the bottom of the heart (130) then represents, without doubt, the beginning of a divine life."

They asked her further whether such a person who loves God wholeheartedly (135) would be better able to handle temptations and the pain of suffering as a result of divine love than a person who experienced such challenges as a result of natural conditions. The lords begged the woman to decide this case. (140) She said: "It might well be that such suffering comes from nature that makes a simple person despair under such a burden. But where you find divine love, (145) there the person will always regard all temptations and all kinds of sorrow as little and insignificant because of God. That person would rather depart from life than expel divine love from the heart." (150)

Then they asked the woman what divine love might be. She said: "Let me tell you honestly, divine love is clarity of the mind, for sure. (155) And divine love is also, I have to say, a reward from God, know this for sure, because God

---

[2] Here is a good case in point. In order to meet the rhyme scheme, the child refers to his mother as "fräwelein," meaning "'Fräulein," or young, virginal, noble lady. This is completely inappropriate in this context; hence my preference for "mother."

does not want to give any other reward but one for love, believe me. The greater your love is for God, (160) the greater will be your reward by God in eternity."

Thereupon they asked her more: "What does God, who is mild and glorious, want to give as a reward after this life (165) to His most beloved friends?" She said: "Allow me to answer you that. God wants to clothe His dearest friends with eternal life, indeed. They will see His wonderful and clear face (170) in eternity together with the angels in the heavenly kingdom."

They asked her what an angel is. The woman answered them openly: "An angel is a noble spirit (175) and a messenger sent by God down here for the sake of our salvation and happiness, and then in return as a messenger from us to God. It is a candle [light] that kindles itself before God, believe me." (180)

Next they asked her what God the Lord is Himself. The woman answered them: "God the Lord is a gift that has to give itself. (185) He is a question that must answer itself. He is a light without smoke that must kindle itself. With these [metaphors] I want to teach you (190) that He is a very clear light that burns and shines forth strongly in all the saints, in the pure angels, and also in the eternal life; (195) all receive great joy from it, which will never exhaust itself."

Further, they asked her what God would be prepared to create (200) eternally, to accomplish constantly and without interruption. The woman answered thereupon: "God does two things without ever letting them go: He raises and lowers the children of the world. He who tries to rise here through arrogance, (205) God mercilessly lowers, and he who lowers himself here on earth through honest humility, him God will truly raise and place among the throng of angels."[3] (210)

At last they asked [her] one more time: "What do the saints and the angels live on in the heavenly kingdom? What do they eat there with joy, or what do they all drink?"(215). The woman, who shone through her pure virtues, answered: "They enjoy as food the beauty of God and are ready to drink His divine love, which is clear and sparkling, of which He will never run out." (220)

Then the woman said politely: "Dear lords, I want to ask you also to share some of your teaching with me, which I will then keep well in my mind." She asked: "What is a person supposed to do here on earth (225) to become worthy to enjoy the brilliant Godhead?" The two clerics gave her the following answer: "The person must do the following: (230) Pray devoutly and confess openly; speak little, and then only with an intelligent mind; and be happily obedient. Be poor willingly, (235) be simple in mind with a kind attitude. Peace ought to be poured into the heart, and the heart ought to be peaceful, protected by virtues. The heart also ought to be humble, not caring for temporary goods. (240) Furthermore, the heart ought to be filled with sorrow over the torture that Jesus

---

[3] Again, the masculine pronoun really includes both genders. It would be too clumsy to try to be overly gender neutral and create stylistic stumbling blocks that Kaufringer himself did not intend.

Christ had to suffer, since our Lord says: 'In that person who keeps my torture in mind (245) and locks it into his heart, I will bloom in silent secrecy as the noble tree does in the month of May.' The person who avoids arrogant language will not cause any damage to others (250) and will keep quiet in the name of God. That is more significant before God than to jubilate together with all the angels for the whole day. (255)

The person who keeps quiet for an hour in the name of God, and yet would have liked to talk, spills much of his own blood through this pain. (260) That person then can say happily to Christ the God in the heavenly kingdom: 'Lord, You spilled Your blood on my behalf, and so I have spilled my blood for You, giving it freely, (265) when I repressed my words.' For the person who undergoes an hour in pain and willingly accepts opposition, or refrains from arrogance, (270) not doing anything wrong against another person in the form of deeds, intentions, or words, although the other has hurt him, that is, for the person who displays such patience, an hour of such behavior is better (275) than that he aim for the goal of praying intently for twenty hours from the bottom of the heart. That person gains more grace that way than from flagellating and beating oneself (280) for twenty hours so that the blood runs from the shoulders down the back, since patience in the sight of suffering is the treasure of virtue (285) and earns much reward in the face of God."

After the woman had listened to the words of the praiseworthy priests, she thanked them deeply from her heart. She said: "You have given me a lesson (290) that I will never be able to forget. You have also let me know much through your teaching and your good words about suffering and recalcitrance. Indeed, I know very well (295) that I am tortured here by my husband, the miller. He will soon arrive here with the ass and I will have to help him (300) in lifting down the bag. I must ask you to leave now; I can no longer talk with you. I will keep you in my prayers from now on without stopping (305) because of your virtues and wise teaching. May God protect you!" She loyally entrusted the two men to God's blessing. Thus they both left from there. (310) They might well have been two angels, sent by God in the shape of people to the miller's wife, indeed. Thus spoke Heinrich Kaufringer.

Misericord in the Cathedral of Ulm, Germany

No. 18: *The Devil and the Wandering Scholar*

Once someone asked me and wanted me to tell him openly what in this world would be the worst against which none would be able to resist. (5) I told that man: "I know nothing living here on earth that is as miserable as evil old women. No one can tell the full story or write completely (10) about the evilness that fills them. If one of them marries a young man, he must be subservient to her, or she will not allow him to survive. She does this through disgruntlement, (15) which she displays to him all the time through her evilness in all manner, so that he dies early in life. If there are six or seven [husbands in a row], they will all be expelled (20) through the woman's evil character. I tell you truly that an evil old woman quickly chases away [even] the evil devil and does not allow him to stay with her (25) when she shows her horrible character, as I will prove to you now.

Once an old woman owned much money. She was excessively evil and mean. A young man (30) who was clever and attractive wooed her. He took, on the grace of death, that terrible woman as his wife. He suffered badly from his wife's fighting, (35) and he almost fell gravely ill from his grief and might have lost his life. The devil felt pity for him; he seriously hated that woman (40) because she had almost killed the attractive young man with her terrible meanness. Now listen to what the devil did. He transformed into a young man (45) as skillfully as he could. He asked the evil wife right away to marry him. The woman was not opposed to it. (50) She accepted him as her husband, which pleased the evil devil, because he wanted to avenge the young man from the woman. He caused her much suffering. (55) When the woman realized that he was always cross with her, she quickly repaid him with her extreme meanness. She also caused him much pain (60) through many sharp and hard words. Often she beat him on his back and pulled his hair, until finally he fled from her. His strength was weak-ened; (65) the woman had triumphed over him. He departed from her quietly and silently in the shape of a young man. He was in a hurry to leave that woman, because he was afraid she would run after him. (70)

When he came to the open field he immediately noticed that someone had followed him. That person was a wandering scholar. When they met, (75) they agreed to share good companionship in the name of good fortune. The devil told the scholar that he was an evil spirit (80) and that the horrible woman had so ter-ribly mistreated his young, proud body that he had to escape from the woman's fighting and belittling strategies. [1] (85) The student replied right away: "Since you are the devil, I will enjoy having you from now on as a companion." The devil said: "Let us go together (90) to the town in front of us. There is a high-ranking king who has a sweet and fine daughter. I want to go into her. She will lose her mind, for sure. (95) Then you must say publicly that her body is occupied by evil spirits and that you could help her become well. Then they will give you much money, which you must share with me. (100) If you promise me that, then I'll swear upon my loyalty indeed that I will certainly go out of the beautiful and tender virgin." (105) They made an oath together to keep their promises. The devil intended to stay with the pretty virgin in all eternity (110) so that he would be safe from the persecutions of his old wife; the student did not recognize his plan.

The devil quickly went into the wonderful young woman. (115) This virgin then turned incredibly wild and lost all her beauty. The news spread everywhere in the big city. The student rushed to the court (120) where he saw the virgin. He told the king that she was possessed by the devil, whom he wanted to exorcize with the help of God and with his own skills. (125) He pledged his own head, pawning it there, if he were not able to exorcize the devil. The king was pleased and ordered his people to give the student (130) much money on behalf of his daughter so that he would free her from that pain.

They opened a [special] room into which the student immediately took the young woman by himself. (135) All other people had to stay outside. The student quietly begged his companion with all his might to leave this barrel [body] as he had promised him. (140) But the devil did not want to do that. He thought: "Now I have peace and protection from my horrible wife." The student leaned toward him and said to his companion: (145) "Now demonstrate your loyalty and drive yourself immediately out of this body or I will experience great anxiety because I will lose my head, if you abandon me." (150) He reminded him of their companionship. But no matter what the student said or shouted, both in friendship and in wrath, it was all for nought. The devil wanted to stay in that body. [2] (155)

Because of his fear the student began to perspire, which he could really not help in this emergency. But his clever mind helped him to find a solution (thus he cheated the devil). He stepped out of the chamber, (160) where he found all the people waiting. He said: "You must all hit on the door to this room with great noise and rage. Then I will be able (165) to exorcize the enemy." He returned to the chamber and sat down next to the virgin and wanted to beg the devil once again. Now, all the people approached (170) the door with great noise, making a huge din in the entire castle. They screamed loudly. The devil, filled with great fear and horror (175) said to the student: "What is happening there in the house?" The wandering student replied: "Honestly, I tell you, and swear upon

---

[1] Literally: "shame," meaning that she embarrassed him or caused him shame.
[2] Literally: "possess that barrel."

my body, your old wife is coming here with great noise. (180) She is happy to have found you at this place. She wants to take you home with her, and intends to fetter you so that you can never escape again." (185) The devil became terribly frightened and did not want to await the wife. He rushed, as his fear made him do it, into the depth of hell. Nevertheless, even there he worried (190) that he might not be secure from that evil woman in hell.

I tell you honestly, nothing is meaner in this world than a miserable old, evil woman (195) who, with her disgusting body and with her false mind, terrifies even the evil devil, who is properly called the worst creature. She causes him much pain and shame (200) and creates great worry in him. That's what Heinrich Kaufringer is saying.[3]

---

[3] It was a common motif in late-medieval literature to denigrate old women in a brutal fashion; see the contributions by Gretchen Mieszkowski and Karen Pratt to *Old Age in the Middle Ages*, 2007.

No. 19: *Turning Away from the World*

Upon my oath, I advise you all that the person who does not want to suffer from hellish pain should turn away from the world and escape from all material goods, because this life is filled with much evilness, (5) shame, and evil games, lack of loyalty, and much terrible intrigue. The child opposes the father, and brother fights brother. Wherever I look in the world (10) I observe nothing but cunning. One person causes damage to another through evil words where he does not hear it [talks behind his back], through which he destroys his honor, but talks in a friendly manner when facing him. (15) The world is filled with woes. The prophet Josiah says in his book: "Depart from Babylon, if you want to preserve your soul well." (20) With that he meant the unclean world since it hands out ill-earned money, through which the soul gets into trouble. John also tells us the truth: "Those people live in great unrest [war] (25) who are willing to live in this world." Whoever turns away from the world and flees toward God through a pure life will find peace, I assure you. There where you find peace is also God. (30)

St. Augustine informs us: "Woe to you who love this world, you are looking for life in the land that is called death. There you truly do not find respite." (35) While you lean toward the enjoyment of that life in which you will be burdened by worries [labor], it might be possible that you much prefer that [other] life (40) in which there is no pain or mourning, only delight and joy at all time. Whoever sees his house burning down rushes to escape from it so that he does not suffer harm. (45) Similarly, people constantly burn without fail in the fire of unchastity. That lust misleads people greatly, and the fact that they cannot flee from it is a terrible strike against the soul, (50) causing an eternal loss.

You can also recognize the danger of this world in natural things. When the quality of wine wanes while kept in the barrel, (55) nothing can help it then except to pour it immediately into another barrel before it loses all of its strength. Similarly a human being is endowed (60) with wealth and great power, with many different joys of this world. Through those things evilness sneaks up on him and virtues move away. Thus the person destroys the soul, (65) unless you protect yourself and flee from this world and move into another barrel in which there is no unclean yeast to attack the virtues.[1] (70) That means, decide to lead a clerical life, where you will exist much better without fear and the pain of worry.

---

[1] The narrator continues with the wine metaphor for human life.

The person who loves the dangerous world (75) loves his own murderer. Saint Augustine says: "Love the world without any weariness [hatred], and it will devour you right away and you will end up in hell." (80) [For instance:] The disloyal Judas had come to the Jews and had betrayed [Jesus] to them, saying: "The one whose lips I will kiss, do not let him get away from you (85) and surely take him away so that he cannot escape from you." In the same way the unclean world certainly speaks to the devils: "Him whom I kiss now, (90) granting thus fortune and dignity, as I tell you honestly, he is the right one, apprehend him; never let him escape from you and firmly take him away with you. (95) Make sure that he does not lose his good luck [here in this life], then he will be yours and subsequently belong to the throng of devils."

I also want to compare the world with the game of chess, (100) in which there are kings, knights, and pawns. When the game is about to come to an end, it continues much longer through the actions of the king and the knights. They uphold the gains of the game (105), even when the pawns are lost. When the game is over, all figures earn the same destiny [get the same advice]: the king, the knights, and the pawns are put away (110) in a bag without any differentiation. Both the king and the knights drop to the bottom of the bag because of their weight, while the pawns rest on the top (115) within the same bag. Likewise the world concludes the same way as the chess game.

There are kings, knights, and servants, some tall and others small, some bent over and others straight, (120) some nobles and others peasants, some poor and others rich. They live in an unequal fashion. One wields more power than thousands next to him. They play the game fully informed[2] (125) until checkmate has been spoken. Thus the game comes to an end; that means, when death arrives they all will be put away in the deep bag of earth, (130) both the knight and the peasant lying together. If the king had been short of virtues while he was alive, he must drop into the fire of hell and is placed at the bottom of the bag (135) because of the weight, which he created insofar as he was filled with evilness and void of good deeds. Since the world thus passes away and those people have no use of it (140) who are committed to it, they are void of reason, who are ready to serve the world. It is the death-trap for the children of this world (145) who enjoy its pleasures.

The person who wants to be dedicated to this world will receive a reward like the treatment given a violin. It sings sweetly and beautifully (150) the whole day until evening. When she receives money as a reward, people take it away from the violin and put that very reward into an old bag. (155) Similarly, people are clad in an old shroud when they die. That's [all] that follows them from this world into the grave. Nothing of the person's properties (160) and labors follows him [into the grave], only the shroud. Even his deeds do not follow him when

---

[2] Literally: "with the full advice."

Wooden bridge, Lucerne, Switzerland, with guard tower

he steps out of this world. If those had been good here in this life, (165) then the soul will prosper (survive) in front of God. When the deeds had not been good, the soul will have to suffer for eternity in the fire of hell. Heinrich Kaufringer is saying that.

No. 20: *The Paid Lawyer*

An evil custom that one has to hire lawyers has emerged in Bavaria and in other lands; I am not pleased with that. In cities where that happens (5) the laws become undermined by those very lawyers when they burden the people with their great and painful fees, when one is in need of them as spokespersons, (10) Now, you can often find a stupid man who raises his voice and wants to be a lawyer, for which he charges people, although he cannot speak well (15) and is void of all wisdom. He then causes [through his bad defense] the other to lose the house, the fields, and whatever he owns. That lawyer is too expensive. There are many who can talk well (20) and twist words just as you want only as long as you pay them much. Such a one knows how to undermine everything, how to transform right into wrong. When you grease his hand [bribe him], (25) how quickly he then makes it so that the wrong becomes right!

Similarly he makes the crooked straight and the straight crooked by means of his tongue, which is false and stupid. (30) He does all that [just] for payment. When someone has a case and tells him all about it, whether it is strong or weak, such as when he has little chance to win the trial [does not have much evidence to support his case], (35) the disloyal man still inspires with comfort and legal advice until he has convinced the good man through his words to hire him immediately (40) and promise to pay him. But it might happen that the same man faces an opponent who also tries his good luck and follows the same lawyer's advice. (45) To whomever can pay more money he offers his help. When the second man then approaches him and gives him more than the first person, he works skillfully (50) to abandon the first man, although he has received payment from him, helping the second man in his plight because he gave him more money.

I have heard the following true story. (55) Once two neighbors fought openly against each other over a dripping container that constantly caused much damage on a wall. One of them was a shoemaker, (60) the other, a furrier. The shoemaker did not shy away from going to a smart lawyer to whom he revealed the injury he incurred (65) and for which the furrier was responsible on a daily basis. The shoemaker brought a pair of good boots with him and said: "Dear Sir, take these (70) and be my spokesperson before the court." When the lawyer heard that, he answered that he would help him, and took the gift from him.

He went to court (75) and with clever words advocated well for the shoemaker to his advantage. When the furrier noticed that the shoemaker gained the upper hand through his smart lawyer, (80) he became deeply frightened. His

friends arrived and openly said that the law had been bent through their delib-
erations [the shoemaker's and the lawyer's]. (85) The furrier was pleased to hear
that because he would almost have failed. He thought: "How can I arrange to
have the lawyer take up my cause? Otherwise I will suffer great danger." (90) He
immediately made a fine coat out of good cloth lined with the soft skin of a fox.
He carried it with him when he went to the lawyer's house. (95) He said: "Sir,
take this small gift and do not reject it; do not be hateful against me as you were
before."

The lawyer was not a fool (100) and took the bribe gladly. He said to the furrier: "I will not cause you further harm; just go home and do not worry."

Now, the day arrived (105) when the court convened. The shoemaker arrived believing that his case was a finished deal, but it became bad and crooked,
because his lawyer had become lame [ignorant] (110) through the furrier's gift.
He began to destroy the shoemaker's case with his false and evil words. He intended nothing but to cause damage to the poor shoemaker, (115) to make him
lose money and honor. He manipulated the laws and defeated the shoemaker,
who thus lost a great fortune. (120)

The shoemaker became quite distraught then and returned to his lawyer, vis-
iting him in his home. He said: "My dear sir, you promised me too much before.
(125) Truly, I say, it seems to me that you did not protect me. I did not spare my
goods; instead I shared something of them with you. But you gave me an evil return. (130) Earlier I would have won the law case, but today you were a fool and
lost my case." The lawyer responded wrathfully: "Return quickly to your own
street (135), the fox has devoured the goat" [idiomatic].

Thus the shoemaker was badly deceived. The valuable boots did not help, because the coat lined with fox skin reduced them to nothing. (140)

Indeed, there are evil lawyers who have an evil mind when they demand a
reward for transforming rightfulness to its opposite. When he defends someone
at court, a virtuous lawyer (145) always remembers to listen only to him and pursue a just case, without allowing anyone to weaken his stance. (150) But when he
[who is seeking a judgment] is not in the right, then he [the lawyer] immediately
alerts him to that fact and does not manipulate that case. That's what is called a
just court.

That lawyer is virtuous and good (155) who does his job in the name of God
and not by way of a deceptive strategy. God will reward him fully with much
more than worldly goods.

The courts are well protected (160) in some imperial cities, for sure. The
best of them have to be ready throughout the year at all times to give judgment
without evil intent. The person who then brings a suit to them (165) will not be
charged by the courts; instead they are doing their job completely in the name
of God. Thus they do not become the object of mockery, as is the case in those
countries where judgment is reached through [secret] payment. (170) When a
virtuous person decides to become a lawyer in the name of God and not in return

for money, people will not respect him as much as before.[1] (175) But where lawyers are not paid and custom rules that the best from the city council happily
serve as lawyers in the name of God, they receive much honor. (180) That is, indeed, a good custom because there is not disloyalty such as where false lawyers
[chatterboxes] deceive both old and young when they receive money for their
counsel. Heinrich Kaufringer is telling you that.

---

[1] Here is a contradiction in the text. Kaufringer argues in vv. 171–75 that an honorable person who takes up the task as a lawyer without payment will not enjoy as much
public respect as before. But then in vv. 176–80 he emphasizes that people greatly honor
those lawyers who work for free. The solution seems to be that in the first case he refers
to an ordinary person assuming the task of a lawyer; in the second, he specifies a member
of the city council.

No. 21: *The Half Blanket*[1]

Holy Scripture teaches us that God will grant a long life to the person who honors his father and mother [Fourth Commandment]. Moreover, God will give that person as reward the privilege of joining the throng of angels. (5) But I have often noticed, as you can unfortunately observe many times, what [today] happens in the world: a child causes his father much dishonor and even pain. (10) When the father reaches old age, then the son pays little attention to being loyal and makes his father's life miserable. This once occurred. There was a very rich man (15) who abandoned his father when he had become incapacitated. The father suffered much from the cold; hunger and thirst tortured him. Frost and cold snow (20) and other misfortunes surrounded the old man. Irrespective of his sorrow and pain, none of it concerned the son.

Now, that rich man had a pleasant son (25) whom he treated very well and whom he loved dearly without end. He was about ten years of age. When the cold winter had arrived (30) and his grandfather, the old man, wore very little clothing, the child often went to him and witnessed his misery. (35) The old man said to the grandson: "I beg you, my dear child, plead with your father, who will not refuse you anything, to consider my sorrowful state (40) and help me out of it. The frost threatens to kill me; ask him to get me a simple coat; God will protect you for that."

The child went to the father (45), hugged him tenderly, and spoke in sweet terms to him: "Dear father, listen to my words and my request. My grandfather suffers from sorrow (50) and is in great discomfort. When I saw him recently, he was not well dressed. He suffered pain from the frost, which caused me to pity him. (55) I beg you, dear father, that you show, on my behalf, your loyalty and clothe his body so that he can fend off the frost." (60)

The father was very pleased with these words.[2] To tell the truth, he bore hatred against his own father. But out of love for the child he did the following: he quickly bought a blanket (65) with which to cover his father during the cold winter. The poor man was very happy about that.

---

[1] In the source for this story which Kaufringer used, "The Half Blanket A," the son receives a blanket and cuts it into half, giving one half to the grandfather and keeping the other for his own father in his old age, hence the explanation for the title, which is somewhat inappropriate for Kaufringer's text. For version A, see *Erzählungen des späten Mittelalters*, vol. I, 93–97.

[2] A rather contradictory comment here.

When the child saw the blanket, he said to his father (70): "Really, I will not let it go, you must fulfill my request: I need to have the same kind of blanket as my grandfather." The father said: "No, dear child! (75) I will give you nice, beautiful, and elegant clothes in plenty. Those are much more fitting for you than this rough and hard blanket, which would hurt your body." (80) The child did not want to accept that; [instead] he insisted on getting the same blanket as the one that his grandfather had received.

When the child had that blanket, (85) he told his father what he wanted to do with it. He said: "I do not want to use this heavy blanket for myself. I want to keep it safely and well protected (90) until you turn old and have become as weak [sick] as my grandfather is right now. Then I want to cover you with this rough blanket (95) as a protection from the frost your weak body. Thus I will treat [reward] you the same way as you have treated my grandfather; I will not grant you better clothing." (100)

The man became deeply frightened about that. He reflected back and forth that he had not treated his father, the weak man, in a friendly fashion, and he regretted it greatly. (105) Through the words and teaching of his child he was reminded to nourish his father better with food and good, clear wine until his death, (110) and he took good care of him so that he did not suffer any shortage. He honored him greatly.

With this story we learn that we do not earn misfortune (115) if we listen to children [become like children]. As a consequence we ought to treat father and mother well in return for the reward that God will grant us so that we will enjoy a long life [here on earth], (120) and beyond that an eternal life. Heinrich Kaufringer is telling you that.

No. 22: *The Good Deeds*

A person asked me to explain a situation.[1] Since an individual lives in sin and clearly perceives that he cannot abandon the sinful life and is afraid of sinking ever deeper all the time, (5) how then would good deeds help him, along with devotional prayer, fasting, and giving of alms? So I should let him know what good deeds would (10) help him and how they would be useful.

I said: "I will let you know. Holy Scripture clearly tells us: God does not pay attention to the sinner when he maintains the will to sin (15) and does, at the same time, good deeds. The latter action won't be useful in reaching the heavenly kingdom. The devil will garner the soul if he acts like that without contrition. (20) Further, in another passage you can read that God does not neglect to reward any good deeds that are done here on earth for His sake. Therefore, I tell you honestly: (25) good deeds help the sinner in a threefold manner. When he is suffering in the fire of hell, the pain is reduced on behalf of his good deeds, because I find it written that there are many different types of suffering and locations in the depth of hell (there are both young and old people [souls]) next to his own. (35) Everyone has to suffer sorrow, and everyone feels pain according to his own guilt.

The other thing God does for the sinner as a result of his good deeds (40) is that he receives here in this life from God wealth and the rewards of good fortune so that the world loves him. (45) God grants him all that as a reward for his good deeds. People then pay him great respect and credit him with much worth.

Let me then tell you the third reward. (50) If you receive that, it is the best, namely that God resides in the person and protects him and sustains his life here until he begins to resist sin and turns to God, (55) so that he finishes his life completely according to God's will. The person will protect himself through full repentance, leading to the dissolution of his guilt, and thus will earn God's grace. (60) All his good deeds from long ago, which had been [seemingly] dead because of the sins, will come then to his good use, because he has the will to turn away from sin. (65) All the deeds will bear [good] fruit and will profit [him].

"The person who is stuck in sinfulness and increases it on a daily basis in his mind without every turning back (70) and yet also does good deeds besides,

---

[1] The narrator uses the term "mär," which carries so many different meanings, from "adventure story," "verse narrative" (genre), "amazing account," or "situation" to "condition," if not simply "news."

receives three types of rewards, at least one or more. But truly blessed is the person who receives the final reward, (75) gaining eternal salvation. The other two rewards, however, deprive the sinner of eternal life without doubt. Heinrich Kaufringer is telling you that."

No. 23: *Merchants in Disagreement*

Nothing is worse, as far as I can tell looking over all the world—in cities, in markets, in all the countries—hence nothing is worse by which people suffer damage and shame and more misfortune (5) than when people are not of the same opinion. This results in discomfort and lamentable woes. Then misfortune (10) strikes them with great wrath and people often lose their lives and goods, and many are robbed of their honor. If people were of the same opinion and walked the path of righteousness, (15) no one would suffer a loss. You can observe in many good cities that people have different opinions; one person leans that way, the other the opposite way. Envy and hatred rule among them; (20) one represses the other. Those who do not have a spokesperson [otherwise: lawyer] often lie at the bottom. You can observe many gaining the upper hand who know how with their intelligence and skill (25) and the support of their friends, to make wrong appear right, and right appear wrong. With his false and ignorant words [tongue] (30) the [lawyer] attracts those who act illegally and meanly. He supports them all the time so his group will be that much stronger. Thereby virtuous people are repressed; (35) they all keep quiet and hide away, and they have to suffer much mistreatment.

Truly, I say: Great trouble comes of it. Each person wants to expel his friend (40) and even destroy him. There are many conflicts when one person judges the other as unworthy. There appear then Guelphs and Ghibelines[1] who never do any good to each other. (45) That city is not well protected where you find such tensions [between political parties]. That is the downfall of the city, because if they encounter war, they cannot succeed (50) since everyone wants to be the lord. When one person is filled with wine, he does not want to obey.

We regularly hear about and read that often (55) the city population retreats and does not win victory in war because of their great disagreements. If people agreed with each other like the members of the court, (60) no one would be able to defeat them or overcome them in any way. Where there is no agreement, killing and murder happen, as I want to teach you. (65)

---

[1] Italian political factions, especially in Florence and northern Italy, from ca. the twelfth to the fifteenth century. The Guelphs supported the Pope, and the Ghibellines supported the Emperor. Both terms are derivatives of German names, the Welfs = Guelphs, and the W[a]iblingen = Ghibellines. See http://en.wikipedia.org/wiki/Guelphs_and_Ghibellines (last accessed on Sept. 5, 2014); see also Oscar Browning, *Guelphs & Ghibelline*, 1894/2011.

Once many fellows gathered on an open field, as I have heard it told. There were about thirty or more of them. They intended to pursue (70) their business as merchants. They owned great numbers of goods and much money. Six robbers who lived in the forest noticed this (75) and arranged a big ambush together with their disloyal counselors, consulting with them on how to go about robbing and grabbing everything by subjugating the merchants (80) and taking all their goods from them. Two of the robbers quickly rode out from their hiding place to the merchants and yelled at them: "Note what we want! We tell you quite clearly, (85) here are four of the count's debtors. He is waiting there in the forest and wants to know whether you are willing to hand them over without fighting and resistance. (90) They have caused him many injuries, and for that reason he does not want to let them escape. If you are willing to obey, then the others can survive. But if you are not willing to do so, (95) you will enjoy neither peace nor respite. You will lose your lives and goods."

Now, the other four companions were hiding and made their presence known (100) skillfully, pretending to be part of a large group. The merchants became very unhappy and stepped together for a council, debating how they should respond. (105) A very wise person was among them. He said: "On my oath, we should all oppose that and not hand over anyone from among us as long as we have our lives and bodies. (110) We should rather succumb to death. Together we will survive or die."

His words pleased all those who were filled with loyalty and upheld their honor. (115) But many others thought about it differently. One among them addressed them all: "I do not want to suffer pain (120) because of another person. I know for sure that I have never done anything against the count. The person who is responsible should live up to his obligation. (125) For sure, I do not want to pay for him." His words appealed to all the other merchants who did not consider the situation properly, as it would develop thereafter. (130) Hence, there was a big division and bickering among them all. But the majority opined that those (135) who had done something wrong against him should suffer pain and misfortune at the hand of the count. Those they were willing to hand over.

The two robber knights [squires; fellows] waited for the outcome. They received this answer: "Take your four culprits (140) and lead them away with you. The others should be left in peace." The two thieves immediately rushed up and quickly noticed (145) who was dressed most richly among the group of merchants. They grabbed four of them, took away their weapons, and fettered their hands tightly (150) so that they would not encounter any danger from them. Then they led them away to their companions waiting in the hiding place. They robbed them of all the goods they found on them. (155) Without delay the two [thieves] returned from the forest to the merchants and spoke to them angrily: "There are still eight who have lost (160) the count's grace and mercy. Indeed, they must do penance for their fault here in this field, or he will come rushing here himself and take all your lives and goods. (165) See over there, he is waiting

in the hiding place with sixty lance carriers and more." All the merchants together became deeply frightened. They knelt down (170) and begged for mercy. The
two robbers did not care about that. They quickly grabbed eight men from among
them, tied their hands as one does with thieves. (175) Then the other companions
came rushing from the hiding place with their sharp lances, hitting and stabbing
them very hard, giving them no chance (180) until the group, which had been
split in their opinions, was completely defeated and all of them suffered losses.
They lost all of the goods that the robbers found on them. (185)

Is that not a great shame? Only six men did that to them. Thus it might happen to those who are not of the same opinion, whether rich or poor, tall or small,
(190) noble or not noble, young or old, or whatever figure they might have, who
always live in such a way that one is opposed to the other. From that many troubles follow, as Heinrich Kaufringer is telling you.

No. 24: *The Evil and Worldly-Wise [Unscrupulous] Counselors*[1]

In old times the world disliked rogues and freeloaders [parasites] and rejected them as disgusting, but now they have gained in popularity and people like and cherish them (5) since their label [name] has changed from being evil to being good. When a person now commits an evil deed, as cheaters and parasites once did, he can step forward and is [as a result of his apparent smartness] being consulted (10) by princes and great lords, so that all other members of courts are subject to them and grant them much honor. This is the result of what they are called [now]. (15)

Now, pay attention as to how the name has changed. Today they are called worldly-wise, clever, and intelligent. That's how they are identified everywhere (20) all over the world. Those who were called rogues and earned their living through flattery [or: deception] now enjoy a worthy name [reputation]. Take note, and do not be blind to it: (25) they are called worldly-wise and clever. People today mean that they are filled with wisdom; yet they are filled to the brim with disloyalty and false teachings, (30) which has nothing to do with wisdom. Wisdom is associated with God, but disloyalty is not part of it, that is, neither cunning nor false counsel. Those who are called worldly-wise (35) today have a life completely filled with disloyalty, which hurts people. They flatter their lords [make themselves loved by them]. When a person does something badly (40) and causes a little damage, they [the evil counselors] make it much worse [make it weak] before their lords through their counsel and false advice.

Many a person loses his wealth and honor when he has only stepped on a chicken. (45) Then he has to pay for this fault a hundredfold. [The counselor says:] "Lord, I am telling you honestly, he has enough money and can pay easily for his crime [guilt]. (50) Don't be sweet and kind. Make certain that people are afraid of you [respect you]." Thus he gives false counsel.

---

[1] "World-smart" would be the literal translation, and although the word does not really exist in the English language according to the OED, it expresses best what is meant here instead of such adjectives as "urbane" or simply "worldly." The narrator means individuals who are very glib about their role in life and understand how to cope in this world effectively to their own advantage. These are smooth profiteers. For practical purposes, however, "wordly-wise" seems the best idiomatic phrase here, as long as we understand the negative connotation.

When a person has a case to bring forward and requests his help, (55) he will refuse to do so until he is pleased with his payment. I mean the evil deception on which he is fully focused. He makes sure that his lance does not burn [idiomatic: that he does not incur any loss] (60) since he knows how to arrange matters so that he receives only profit. That way he can show a happy face and present himself in a good light toward all people, (65) both great and small; he smiles at many to whom he would grant nothing good. If someone shows hatred toward him and insults him with a few words, (70) he can well ignore it but in the end pays him back. When that person stumbles and sprains his ankle, he hits him fully on the nose. (75) Thus he redirects the old hatred dangerously and quietly so that no one notices that he has stoked the fire for him [idiomatic: has caused him all that trouble and pain]. No one recognizes his evil character (80) because he displays a pleasant demeanor toward everyone at all times.

I cannot write about those who demonstrate such cleverness in any other way but that in all circles they are called (85) suave and clever people. You find nowadays no other people on earth who are respected as much and are thus dignified (90) as those who are worldly and clever. God must feel great pity that those people who formerly were disregarded completely now enjoy dignity and honor. (95) The pace of the world has slowed tremendously. Just as the crab walks backwards, those who had been behind are now at the front, as I observe in the world (100), insofar as people love evil ones who enjoy a dignified life. I am thinking of the rogues and parasites. Heinrich Kaufringer is telling you that.

No. 25: *The Seven Deadly Sins*

Seven unhealthy weaknesses [sins] are a grave danger to the body. When a person suffers from just one, no one can give him good advice. Even if he does not die from it, (5) he will hardly get away [unpunished]. By the same token, seven sins threaten the poor soul. When a soul is afflicted by one of these sins in this life (10) and remains its victim, it will have to suffer eternal pain [in hell], condemned to stay there without [any hope for] an end.

When the heavenly Father observed (15) that human beings were sick and weak, chased away from God's grace and expelled from Paradise, burdened by sinfulness that made the soul unhealthy, (20) He wanted to chase away the danger of these sins. Therefore he sent to the soul for its salvation the Holy Spirit as its consoler, to provide medicine for the soul through His seven [heavenly] gifts. (25) These chase away from the soul all the pain, all the sins and all the heavy burdens. I mean the Seven Deadly Sins, through which the soul is heavily burdened and is eternally troubled. (30)

Now, let me tell you honestly of the heavy physical suffering and the great seven illnesses that deprive a person of his health. The first illness is this kind: (35) often one sees people who have blisters and wounds on their body. I have read about this and have written that these swell up extremely. People experience much suffering from them, (40) as I can tell everyone. If they disappear from the body, then one clearly notices that the person's sickness is gone and healed. (45) If the blisters stay with him, as we read [in the sources], then that person dies. This sickness[1] is meant as a symbol of vanity, which swells up and wounds the person (50) and makes the heart boastful. He no longer wants to recognize those whom he had known before. Thus the "nice" Lucifer lures many people away from the heavenly throne (55) down into the depth of hell. That sickness is a blow to the soul that could cause it injury. If it remains and does not let go of the poor soul, (60) then the soul departs from this life and is handed over to eternal death. When that sickness swirls and blows away, then the soul is immediately healed. (65) Then the Holy Spirit becomes a good medical doctor for the soul. It grants the soul a small bandage, the gift of divine fear that always (70) chases away the ulcer of arrogance from the heart.

Next I tell you about the other sickness that burdens the human body. That is the unclean leprosy. (75) Whoever is affected by leprosy should not share any

---

[1] The poet suddenly switches from plural to singular here.

abode with a woman or a man because he poisons the clear air with his breath. (80) When that sickness strikes the air, it affects healthy people, who are then infected as well. With that reference we are meant to understand envy and hatred, great dangers for the soul. (85) Whoever is overcome by them also should not share his life with women or men, because he is poisoned so terribly through his evil mind (90) that he plots with his words, mind, and sense, as a snake does, by which people are hurt.

The Holy Spirit provides good medicine to the soul completely free of poison against this danger. (95) These gifts [the medicine] are goodness and mercy. The soul becomes clear and healthy from them, because the gifts quickly chase away hatred and poisonous skin, (100) which empty the soul from that poison and fills it with purity.

The third sickness brings little profit or use. It is called "frenesis" [phrenitis] (105) I will translate the word for you into German: the person afflicted by it rages and rants all the time and is void of his reason. By this I mean wrath, (110) which is a heavy burden for the soul. He rages and screams all day and leads a crazy life filled with insanity [wrath].

To fight against it the Holy Spirit arrives (115) in the soul many times together with the gift of divine art. That art can soften and completely chase away the sharp rage so that the person becomes sane again. (120) After all, a person who has opted for the divine art cannot be filled with evil rage.

The fourth weakness, absence of joy, which often causes sorrow for the body, is called paralysis. (125) This is a sick person stuck to his bed.[2] The person afflicted by it has his limbs tied together so that he cannot do anything for himself. He lies like a prisoner both day and night (130) and has so little control over his own body[3] that he would burn in a fire before he could crawl away from it. Let us understand the meaning of this paralysis, which is a heavy sickness. (135) It causes great loss to the soul because it hurts and weakens it and makes the individual disinclined toward all spiritual matters, so that he moves away from them. (140)

The Holy Spirit then, as a countermeasure, provides the soul with medicine consisting of the pure gift of its strength. The person infused with it gains so much strength in his mind (145) that he endeavors to do good deeds busily and at all times. Thus laziness is chased away.

The fifth sickness is called "idropisis": that is, a heavy burden for the body. (150) By this I mean people who suffer from hydropsy [dropsy]. Those who suffer from that sickness feel thirsty all the time. With this is circumscribed the sin of greed. (155) He who is constantly greedy and thirsty in his mind, thinking about

---

[2] The original reads: "pettris," which does not exist in any dictionary. But there is the Middle High German word "betterise," which means "sick person," "a person stuck to his bed." Sappler, *Indices*, does not include any entry for this word, let alone an explanation.

[3] Literally: "His self-help is so expensive."

how to gain wealth and fill his money bag so that his treasure chest is full (160) by means of usury, experiences a heavy blow to the soul. He thinks about gaining more both day and night. The consoler of the soul works against it, giving the soul the necessary medicine, offering divine advice, which is the pure gift. (165) That relieves the soul well because it admonishes a person to share some of his goods with the neighbor next to him, whom he recognizes as poor. (170)

As to the sixth sickness, let me tell you about the body's suffering and pain. It is a heavy illness for lords, who are especially afflicted by it. It is called the "[Wer]Wolf" (175) [lycanthropy]. He who observes this phenomenon in himself will eat his own flesh. If he wants to overcome this wrong with good fried meat, as lords eat it, (180) prepared with pure medicine, he must put off that pain in which the sickness resides. When he begins to eat, he is satisfied with it. (185) He leaves his flesh alone, feeling remorse and keeping a distance. When the meal is eaten, he eats his own flesh again. This represents our gullibility. (190) The one person obsessed with gullibility disregards everything he has consumed before. He fills his stomach every day with wine and good food (195) until he has squandered his fatherly inheritance. He has to live the life of a beggar when no one wants to give him credit. Then he must suffer great pain and eat up his own body, (200) [meaning] he is devoured by his own hunger and suffers a miserable death. Against that [sickness] people receive a gift of divine inspiration as medicine for the soul through the influence of the Holy Spirit. (205) After all, God's understanding makes the heart pure and clean, so that God can recognize and perceive it. The person who directs his mind (210) toward drunkenness will not recognize God because his heart is alienated from Him, as you read it in the prophetic texts, such as Hosea (215), who wrote: "Wine and drunkenness diminish the heart" [4:11]. That means: "Wine and drunkenness rob the heart of its clothing." These are the words of virtues and dispel the force of drunkenness. (220)

The seventh pain and sickness that often troubles the body and makes it sick is shaking and rattling. It is an evil habit that often makes the body sick. It occupies a person so much (225) that he can no longer digest well. His throat is so wounded that he desires only what is hurtful to him and weakens him, although he thinks it to be good and pleasant in taste. (230) That which would be advantageous to him appears void of good taste and is objectionable.

What I mean here is the lack of chastity. The person afflicted by it (235) thinks that chastity and pure life are very hard to achieve. By unhealthy food I mean clothing that dresses an evil lack of chastity, which seems a joy and sweetness to him. (240) He is so much filled with evilness that he cannot digest it well, unless the Holy Spirit comes to his rescue with his gifts and helps him to overcome that sickness, applying divine wisdom, (245) which always clears the

Harbor in Ghent, Belgium

heart's throat.[4] That then changes one's mind, turning it away from physical desire. One can then push it far away. (250)

Divine wisdom guides you so that you always turn your mind to good and pure deeds. Thus man becomes well again. He resides so much in virtue (255) that he spends his time there joyfully and is emptied of all evilness. Heinrich Kaufringer is telling you that.

---

[4] Curious and almost inexplicable metaphor, but the original text clearly says: "die den rach des herzen dein / zuo aller zeit rainigen tuot." Perhaps he wants to imply "the mouth of the heart."

No. 26: *The Worldly Sorrows*

I thought by myself, considering evil and good, that God loves nothing more, cherishes nothing more here in this world and in our time than a person who experiences suffering (5) and withstands it with patience. These are the correct roads and paths and the most direct routes leading to the gate of heaven. God will protect people who experience suffering (10) and maintain a happy mind, both here and there because they belong to the select few.

God is so mild and kind that when He sees His friends in this life (15) experiencing pleasures in the world, then He puts thorns on the street and sets up countless troubles in every corner, whether the friends like it or not, (20) so that He does not lose them. Observing His fatherly duties, He strews all their paths with suffering so that they cannot direct their feet in the direction of their hearts' desires (25) and follow only their thirst for divine love. In such a way God captures His friends with all kinds of suffering, since otherwise they would be alienated from God.

Suffering here on earth is a heavy burden, (30) but it creates a space [for us] in eternity [in the heavenly kingdom]. Suffering is such a precious thing that no one can repay God [fully]. Once a person humbly begged God for the experience of suffering for a hundred years. (35) Yet, he was not worthy of God granting his wish to be fulfilled. Suffering supersedes red gold [in value]. The person who recognizes the usefulness of suffering should accept it happily from God's hand (40) instead of another gift. Suffering is the soul's refreshment [nourishment], protects its humility, is a protector of purity, (45) and delivers eternal bliss.

Certainly nothing is more painful here in this life than suffering. Hence you cannot be happier than when you have experienced suffering. (50) Suffering lasts only a short time and gives a long-term experience of love, as I understand it. The person who undergoes forty years of suffering (that's really a short time, compared to life in eternity) [55] will receive as his reward a truly long life that will last for eternity. A person who might be willing to gamble a limited time on earth against eternity should rather try to rest for a hundred years (60) in a fiery oven instead of forgoing the least reward in eternity that is being prepared for him for the least form of suffering here. (65) While the former has an end, the latter lasts forever.

In this world suffering is regarded as an expression of sinfulness, but in the eyes of God it is an immeasurable dignity. It quenches God's wrath and helps to acquire His grace. (70) The person who experiences suffering is abandoned by

his friends wherever he goes, yet he walks on the right path, increasing God's
grace. Suffering produces in people (75) the power to recognize themselves and
to believe their neighbors. Suffering initiates the removal of a person's horrible
misdeeds.[1] Suffering reduces the time spent in Purgatory; (80) it chases away
temptation and removes afflictions, as you can read in documents. Suffering also
renews the spirit and creates much true confidence. Suffering makes your conscience good (85) and creates constant joyfulness in your mind. Suffering is a
healthy drink and a healing herb without doubt, better than all the herbs growing in Paradise. Suffering is a punishing stick (90) that chastises the body, which
has to rot away afterwards anyway, through repentance and feeds the noble soul
well, which will live forever. The soul becomes green again from great suffering
[?] (95) as the beautiful rose does from the dew in May. Suffering brings about a
wise mind and transforms a highly experienced person into a good one. A person who does not practice suffering does not know of the great use resulting
from it. (100) Suffering is the whip of love, a father's strike of those who are pure
and good, that is, of the elect, I kid you not. Suffering pulls [you up] and forces
people to turn to God, whether they like it or not. (105) The person who happily
accepts suffering will be served quickly by love and sorrow, by friends and foes
undoubtedly.

At first God created suffering from nothing before He allowed His friends
to be free of it, (110) because in suffering all virtues are realized, people are honored, and neighbors are improved, thanks be to God. In suffering, patience becomes a living, docile sacrifice, (115) a sweet taste of noble balsam before divine
eyes. It is an imposing wonder above all heavenly companions [house friends].
People can never gaze too much (120) at a skilled knight in a tournament because of his strong and forceful manhood. Similarly, the entire heavenly throng
gazes altogether at a pure person who has suffered much during his time [here
on earth]. (125) Oh yes, how much joy this person grants to all those who reside
in heaven! They reason, quite clearly, is his suffering, since those heavenly boys[2]
have not dealt with [tried out] much suffering themselves. (130) Therefore they
welcome him graciously. He receives the crown of martyrdom because he chose
to accept suffering here on earth, so he is a companion of the martyrs. To display
patience in suffering (135) is a much greater achievement than that about which
you generally read of individuals ordering the dead to rise or performing other
such miracles. Suffering garners strong praise. Suffering achieves (140) a strong
victory over all enemies.

The person who is tortured here through suffering will have his voice sound
in eternity. He sings a new tune before them all in a sweet sounding tone and
with a free mind, (145) the likes of which none of the good angels can achieve
with their songs, because they have never experienced suffering.

---

[1] Literally: "It robs people of their horrible misdeeds."
[2] He means "angels," but uses the term "boys" here.

It is appropriate to honor the dignified and noble Holy Cross (150) because God died on it. Moreover one should, without cunning, praise and honor suffering, submit oneself to it voluntarily, and ask for it intentionally, (155) since God Himself suffered here in this time [of mankind], truly, for more than thirty years, during which time he never enjoyed one good day. And when He was about to die (160) on the cross, then His death came quickly within half a day. Therefore suffering is holy and honorable, because Christ underwent much suffering here on earth during his whole earthly existence, (165) more than on the honorable Holy Cross. God has not imposed suffering on us as an illusion [image]. Hence he is the brother Christ[3] who suffers patiently. (170)

The people suffering here on earth are called the poor, who are oppressed, but before God they are truly called the blessed children of heaven (175) because they are those selected for the eternal kingdom. This Heinrich Kaufringer is telling you.

---

[3] Not clear whether he means "brother of Christ," "Christ's brother," or "brother Christ."

No. 27: *God's Four Daughters*

God the Father in Eternity has so much love for mankind, bottomless and without end, that he does not intend or want people to die in sinfulness (5) and become victims of eternal death. He grants sinners time and a late due date to free themselves from the unclean dirt [manure] of evil deeds willingly through confession, contrition, and penance. (10)

Now, God has here in this world four types of people, I tell you, who are all called Christians. Let me inform you who they are. The first group consists of all those (15) who are wealthy and powerful here in life. The other group of people comprises those who are blind, crippled, and lame, and other sick people who suffer from poverty, (20) including all those children of the world who are victims of suffering and sorrow. The third group of people is unclean: these are all those who live against God's rules, (25) who do not observe His commandments, and who behave all day and night only according to the devil's advice, without any fear of God. The fourth group consists of (30) all those here in this life who are full of virtue, resist evil deeds at all times, both early and late in the day, stand here free of all disloyalty, (35) and are completely opposed to the deadly sins. They also strive to do what pleases God. The kind and beautiful God has prepared for the four groups (40) specific words so that they can gain [acquire] the heavenly kingdom with Him. God wants to hand these to them if they are willing to receive such gifts. (45)

He has four daughters who are clever and fine. They are clothed beautifully in their virtues and purity. God wants to offer those four daughters as a bride to each group as their own (50) here in this sickly life, if those aforementioned fellows are willing to take them. Now, note and pay attention (55) to what these four daughters are called. The first is called compassion, who is endowed with such virtues that she can evoke pity. God the Lord has assigned her (60) to the first group mentioned above, namely those who are rich and powerful here in this pithy life. God wants to give them that beautiful and fine daughter (65) as a bride so that they become compassionate to the miserable, poor and willingly offer them their goods, which God granted them, as a consolation without any second thought. (70) In that way they will be married to that beautiful and pure woman who is called compassion. Thereby they will be charged to turn to eternal life, (75) which God wants to give them as a dowry.

The other fine and tender daughter is born into a high-ranking family; she is called patience. In all circles of this world (80) there is no virtue as fine as patience in suffering. That daughter God wants to award to the other group, and rightly so, as a legitimate wife without change. (85) The people belonging to that group are the ill people [children] who are burdened with sorrow and live in great poverty, not to mention many other types of suffering. Those, whether young or old, (90) when they are truly patient in poverty and sorrow and face great suffering, prove, indeed, to be fellows of the martyrs. They are assured eternal life. (95) God wants to grant it to them as a reward.

The third daughter shines through her nobility and does well for the third group. To those who commit many misdeeds, constantly strive against God, (100) and are trapped in sinfulness, she is appropriately assigned and chosen as their bride. That noble and attractive daughter is called, as I must tell you her name, (105) contrition and penance. Since these worldly fellows [boys] often and in many ways have angered God, it is my advice and teaching that they turn away from their sinfulness. (110) They should request that beautiful and noble daughter from God as a sweet and delightful bride. He will grant their request if they gain, through her works, (115) contrition, carry out a true confession, and do complete penance, so that God will no longer remember their great and many misdeeds. (120) God willingly wants to grant them entrance to the eternal kingdom as a dowry.

Next let me introduce you to the fourth daughter. God loves her all the time because she is a barrel filled (125) with immeasurable virtues.[1] She is called fear of God. God has established that the person who takes her as his mistress will be so perfect in his virtues through her (130) that he may not commit any sin, neither during the day nor at night. The people in that group know this young woman well. They have pledged to marry her. (135) They think about nothing else than how to carry out service to God and constantly improve their virtues. If they commit sins on a daily basis, they habitually (140) go without delay to the priest to receive complete absolution and do their penance after having performed pure and honest confession. The fear of God, with which they are filled, alone achieves that, (145) so that they guard themselves against misdeeds and practice virtue constantly.

For that reason these people [children] live in the house of the heavenly kingdom. There they have eternal joy without pain. These are the words of Heinrich Kaufringer.

---

[1] As odd as it might sound to our ears, Kaufringer has a preference for this term, "barrel," referring to people. See numerous times previously. Sappler, *Indices*, 39, lists the word "vaß" but he does not explain it.

No. 28: *Disputation with a Jew about the Eucharist*

A smart and learned Jew once tried to convert me away from my Christian faith by means of his deep [probing] questions. He said: "Since God is so great, (5) as people sing about and as you can read, how can He then be hidden in the appearance of a little bread [wafer] that is much smaller than God Himself? Indeed, it seems to be a joke to me (10) and against nature that such a small object could contain within itself something many times bigger."

I said to him: "I am going to tell you, (15) if you are willing to believe me. Nature provides us proof: just as a clear mirror glass contains in its small body a house, a mountain, or a whole city, (20) which you can see completely in the little mirror, so is it also possible that God can hide with His great power (25) in the appearance of the little bread."

The Jew said to me: "How can it be then that the bread is transformed into flesh (30), and also that wine transforms completely into blood on the Holy Altar? In my mind that seems to be completely impossible." I answered him: (35) "But you know well that God has done such things, when He created the first human being, who was called Adam. And He made his body (40) in a masterly fashion out of clay, which was immediately transformed into flesh, bones, and blood. You also know what happened with good Lot's beautiful wife (45) when they fled Sodom. She was foolish and ignorant. When she looked behind herself, her body was immediately transformed into a pillar of salt. (50) Since God had done those two things, it is also possible for Him to transform bread to flesh and wine to blood in His good holy body.

"Let me also explain to you (55) the same by means of reference to natural objects. The steam that emanates from the earth transforms immediately its shape into strong and wild roots.[1] From a strong and tight root grows the trunk. (60) Then the branches sprout. When the weather is good, this body transforms within itself. (65) From the wood arise the flowers, delightful in their appearance, from which grow the fruit, such as pears and delicious apples. Since steam transforms that way (70) into many different shapes as part of nature's character, God may with His power transform much more so and easily the form of bread and the property of wine (75) within His own holy body."

---

[1] He probably simply means water, not steam, although the Middle High German "tampf" specifically implies steam.

The Jew then asked further. He said: "Since the Christians say that God re-sides in that little bread, I feel forced to ask about it; (80) it seems strange to me that God does not disappear because the priests use the little bread on a daily basis. Even if your God would be so big (85) that no mountain all over the world could be compared to Him, He would still have been consumed a long time ago."

I answered the Jew thereupon: "God allows us to enjoy Him daily (90) by the priests here on earth, but He cannot be consumed and does not become di-minished. God is constantly one with Himself and at all time without fail. (95) He never suffers any shortage, as I will teach you by means of an example taken from nature: when you have a burning candle, you can quickly (100) without causing any shortage in that one candle light a thousand other candles or more. Yet the candle does not shrink in size because of kindling others and does not burn up. (105) It remains in its nature complete and whole. Likewise you must understand that God remains unharmed and also is not consumed (110) when the priests use Him. He remains without end completely in His majesty, since it does not diminish."

The Jew asked the fourth question (115) and said: "Since God is being wor-shiped [handled; even bartered] at many places and through many priests' hands quite openly in that bread/wafer, (120) then it seems proven that the Christians have more than one God, which is against the First Commandment and against your own faith." (125) I said: "Listen to my words! I will teach you the correct lesson that there is not more than one God whom every single priest worships here. (130) A parable teaches us the following: When the word 'Jesus' is men-tioned in a loud voice at some place where many people are assembled,[2] then that word enters the ears of all present, (135) those standing in front and those in the back. There are many people there, and yet everyone hears the sound of the same word completely, and yet it is only one word. (140) In the same way God is called here on earth down from heaven every day by many priests far and wide through words and devotion and is worshiped in the bread, (145) and yet there is not more than one God in the hands of all the priests."

The Jew was evil and unclean and said: "I want to prove with a smart reck-oning (150) just this one thing, that you have more than one god, as I know and pronounce. Since the priest worships the bread in which God is blessed and di-vides it up into pieces, (155) your faith is undermined, because you also admit that in every piece of bread God resides perfectly and completely. Since that is supposed to be true (160) and since the number of pieces is infinite, you have, without speaking out loud, more than one God and Lord. Your faith is confused and is, as I see it, worth nothing." (165)

I answered the Jew right away without holding back and said: "You cause me great pain through your lack of faith. Nature demonstrates to us (170) through a

---

[2] Literally: "where many people have their living space."

clever example: a person who looks into a mirror sees his own face in it. When he then decides to break the valuable mirror (175) into many little pieces, both large and small, and thereupon wants to look into each one, he can see his face in each (180) entirely without fail, just as in the clear whole mirror, although it is broken up into many parts. There is just one face. Thus I prove herewith that God is both unbroken and true, complete through and through in every piece of the little bread, and is still only one God." (190)

Thus the Jew acknowledged my victory, but he did not want to become a faithful [Christian] as a result of my words. Instead, he wanted only to remain a heretic, for which he will have to suffer eternal pain. (195) These are the words of The Teichner [Kaufringer].

No. 29: *Fight over Love and Beauty*

A clever woman asked me about the following issue: "Which among two things would be praised more and should receive a crown—love or beauty?" I said: "There is no doubt about it, (5) you ought to consider love the better aspect and you should grant it more worth and honor than beauty, as I am going to tell you. Love has a good pedigree: that it is a praiseworthy virtue. (10) The person filled with virtue is loved by everyone at all times. Thus love develops out of virtue without losing any strength. Beauty [on the other hand,] does not have such qualities (15) because it does not derive from virtue. Beauty is determined by arrogance and pride, both of which buttress it, as I can truly assure you. (20) There has never been a master [teacher] so wise who would be able to find written down somewhere or who would be able to write down himself that many beautiful people are rich in virtue. (25) They allow their beauty to go to their heads and do not want to acknowledge anyone else [respectfully] because of their pride. Wise people hate them for that. There is nothing wrong in praising a beautiful person (30) if he gains people's love through virtue, be it a woman or be it a man."

The woman became very angry about that. Her beautiful color turned pale, and she said wrathfully to me: (35) "The entire world desires beauty. God created beauty Himself. Both men and women smile lovingly at a beautiful person when they see her (40) and say that she is called a true beauty, and that no creature on earth could be compared to her. She is the object of heart-felt desire by all. Whoever looks at a beautiful person (45) sings a song full of praise of her. He wants to gaze at her all the time. For that reason love can never be on an equal level with beauty. Both the poor and the rich, (50) kings and praiseworthy lords, priests, women, and men, and so the entire world desire beauty. Therefore she is better and has more worth than love, without doubt. (55) Wherever you might see a festival or any other joyful event, the beautiful person is consulted [is taken into counsel]. When you want to enjoy life at court, be it much or little, (60) there you find beauty in the most worthy crowd. Everyone notices her and smiles at her with a happy heart. Beauty has clear and marvelous eyes and demonstrates an intelligent demeanor (65) insofar as she knows how to incite love everywhere in people's hearts, and is capable of unlocking beautiful bodies and breasts, pouring lustful desire (70) into them as well. Beauty is the highest crown of the body. Beauty makes the neck white and fine. The face has red lips, ready to be kissed (75) to the other person's pleasure. Then there are two lovely cheeks. It would be impossible for a heart, even if it were more than half dead, not to be troubled by desire. (80) Hence, beauty is the crown of all joys and a sweet reward of courtly love. Love itself cannot be an equal to her."

I said to the lovely person: "It must be the very chest containing all joys (85) when beauty can be joined with virtue, which would be highly praiseworthy. But when you see beauty void of virtues, then she is not love's companion. (90) Such beauty is dangerous; its gleaming color is a deception.[1] It equals, pardon my language,[2] a painted barrel of salt that has a beautiful lid,[3] (95) . . . from which bitterness results.

"Love is clothed with virtue. Love offers delight and goodness; love can chase away sorrow (100); love opens the heavenly kingdom. Beauty angers God; love is wonderfully built on virtue; beauty desiccates [fades away] over night; love is appreciated all over the world (105) when no one desires a beautiful person any longer [when she is old and ugly]. Love is smart and knows that the person who can display love is beautiful enough. It seems to me where there is beauty without true love, (110) she is not treated honorably because beauty alone can never acquire a steady friend, unless there is love besides. You can find enough good people who are sagacious without being beautiful, and who display virtue. Beauty without love is arrogance, pride, and danger."

The Teichner [Kaufringer] is telling you that.

---

[1] The original phrase, "kuntervail," does not exist, but the Straßburg manuscript A offers the alternative spelling of "gunterfeit" and the Karlsruhe manuscript writes it as "kuent'fait" which means "deception" or "falsification," well fitting in this context. Sappler, *Indices*, does not include that term.

[2] Literally: "saying this without any hatred."

[3] Here is a gap in the manuscript, and both alternative manuscripts offer a different narrative sequence.

No. 30: *New Foolishness in Fashion*

You can see many amazing things here on earth, if you are just willing to look. Many serve this world from early in the morning till late in the night and thus hurt their own bodies and goods (5) through their service to the world. The servants of this world display the following external insignia: to please the world they dress like hunters so that one can see their naked asses (10) and how they are built. Previously that was done only by monkeys. Their shoes have long points and look up in such a way that they gaze at their lord [who wears them] (15) and inspect what kind of person he is. You can see that they carry two belts, as maidens once did. One belt is attached to the front so that they can place [saddle themselves] better on the horse. (20) The two belts serve this purpose, one tightly in the front, the other in the back. The worldly fools do it that way today. They now want to have two belts (25) because it seems to look better. They carry knives in a funny way: the handle is placed down and the pointed blade goes up; they all call this the new fashion (30) because they have found that to be new [style]. They have attached it to the sheath. If one might need his knife, then the belt has to be unbuckled and they have to reach under for the knives. (35) That could cause trouble for the lords [since they cannot get quickly to their armor]. If one were to carry the knives in the old fashion, the belt would not have to be unbuckled and the knives would sit better, if events did not turn out well [if there was a need for the knives]. (40) Everything is [now] supposed to look attractive [fashionable].

Little hats suffer badly; they are bent back and forth and folded in many different ways, bottom to top, (45) so that they look fashionable, with the inside on the outside. These fools strut like bulls with their caps, to which they often attach two horns (50) that point up in a crooked way, but they think this is fanciful.

Another person likes the following: he pulls his cap forward, (55) creating a fold and an opening, all of which is supposed to be appropriate. On the back part he places a little hat that is broad-rimmed and has many bands. Let me tell you about that little hat (60) (but I need your permission, if I am to talk about it): it barely sits on the back of the head and is stuck there like cow shit. If they carried it properly, it would be much better. (65) There are many hunters now in this world, since one sees many who carry horns, although they cannot hunt. They want to treat women as if they were bait and walk before them like hunters. (70) In previous times one only saw horns on those who knew how to hunt deer and does in the forest. Now people (75) who wear coats and veils on their heads [women] enjoy spending time in the territories of those animals. They are allowed to hunt those animals. For hunting they have old dogs that never bark loudly. (80) These are old games of love [tricks], of which I will tell you [later]. When they run they do not make much noise and yet people use them for hunting going up the mountain.

The servants of the world do even more. (85) They wear heavy necklaces; just as one puts chains around dogs' necks, so one sees these people walk around with such chains. One might consider them thieves, since they walk in that way to please the world. (90) If their confessors were to tell them to do so in the name of God, they would say: "This will make me a laughingstock of the world. Spare me this penance! If I carry a chain around my neck, people will say that I am bound for the gallows [am a child of the gallow], (95) as is the case with thieves and other criminals." It is a shameful custom; the devil mocks them therewith.

Women imitate them in every possible way. They also enjoy being the servants of the world. (100) They are obsessed with arrogance; they have forgotten women's good behavior. They also want to wear coats for riding and strut around like men. Their dresses have sleeves like those worn by men, (105) embellished with many bands and patches, cut from many differently colored cloths. People give them worldly praise.

You can see many men wearing dresses that people say could be used for the hunt. (110) The sleeves are covered with feathers, as if they intended to fly high or low.

A new dance of worldly love has begun. At such a site you can always see (115) both women and men. If peasants had dared to do anything similar, Neidhart would not have allowed it to pass unnoticed nor have withheld his mockery. (120) If today there would be such a fellow or poet, she or he would say much more about it. The dance is properly called "The Shaker," since women shake as much as the men, (125) with both their upper and lower body parts. They shake back and forth, they move their asses and all their limbs. Thus you see them dancing by way of shaking, jumping on their feet (130) as maidens have often done, accompanying the main shaker and making dancing moves with the feet, as if they were being attacked by gadflies.

You can see them doing many other strange things, (135) which one cannot describe in all details, both women and men. But I better let it go. They would not do anything in the name of God that they [happily] do in order to be praised by the world. (140) Therefore we must regard them as blind with their eyes open and like children in their minds. They see all the time the evil reward the world grants. The world discharges its servants miserably (145) when the time for departure comes. The world pushes them away in its deceptive appearance and rips off the elegant necklaces and whatever else they might have as decoration. The world [then] puts them in a plain dress (150) or an old linen. You can quickly see that it is worthless and that the world does not suffer any loss from it. That way the world dismisses its servants, as all masters do. (155) At the end that is the reward of the world. Once the world turns away from them, the devil's guidance takes over. If those people have served the world well, they receive the deserved reward. (160) The devil brings them many fiery chains with which they have to suffer in infinitude, since it was written as follows: "With what people have committed sins they will have to pay for their misdeeds." (165)

Hence, here is my advice: Let go of the world and love God all the time. He can certainly give us a better reward, which is called eternal life. (170) There a thousand years are shorter than one day in this world, to be sure, because eternal life is without suffering. These are The Teichner's [Kaufringer's] words.

No. 31: *The Councilors in the Cities*

Councilpersons in cities should give the best possible advice, which would please me much, but to my regret they do this rarely. The city pays for that in terms of dignity and honor. (5) Unless they change, the situation does not look good to me. They play their secret games when the lords spend time in the countryside, and act shamefully and against the law. (10) When the lords return to the city, the councilors pay them great respect and welcome them sweetly, offering them good wine. I am not happy (15) that they only talk [idly]. They should give advice, I tell you, for the communal good and reputation. But they are very lazy in that regard. They rather enjoy doing something else. (20) They give advice day and night about how each person can get his own cut. They also present themselves as weak, because when there is a small case that a person brings to court (25) they call upon the old counsel (which is too difficult for people who do not have lawyers) and put smartness and craftiness to work. But they often advise according to whom they favor (30) and how they feel about the man. They punish a person who knows how to talk well [much] and has never done anything evil except for a few words uttered and take his goods from him as punishment, (35) That is the way they act and what mindset they have. They let people who should do a penance and are evil go scot-free and do not harm them, though they are worse than thieves. That is the advice they give each other in mutual support. (40) It might happen, after all, that they want to be paid back. Before one of them abandons the mutual interest, they are rather willing to break the law. Here I refer to the small council (45) [lower ranked city council], which wields the authority/power. It is composed of not more than three members. The others sit also at the council but are dull in their wits and probably half childlike, (50) since they hardly give advice. They only notice when someone advises to their disadvantage; then they oppose it immediately. Subsequently they leave things standing (55) and turn to other matters.

Those who would be proper for the council are not listened to. Some give good advice, but then that comes too late (60) and their advice is not followed. Some councilors [young fellows] also attend whose advice is adhered to much more closely. Others sit there quietly. (65) When they are asked: "Do you agree with that?" and requested to speak, they only say: "Yes, everything my lord has said pleases me and seems to be good advice." (70)

This is true and not my imagination. These are The Teichner's [Kaufringer's] words.

No. 32: *The Twelve Properties of Wine*

People say that stones, roots, and [magical] words contain great power because of their virtues. This has been described by the learned masters, but they have not known what miracles come with wine. (5) The person who consumes it in large quantity experiences the greatest of all wonders. It frees me from melancholy, as if I were a bird. Its strength does me only good. (10) It serves me well with or without my thanks.

The first glass of wine that I drank in the evening had the power to quench my thirst. I said in a happy mood, without any evil thought[1], (15) "Blessed be the location where this savior has grown!" More I did not need to say. The second glass of wine had a different quality. Indeed, I gave it credit for its mastership (20) over all the sweet wines, even over the Muscat wine. I said: "Give me it, and fill the glass!"

The third glass of wine was then handed to me, which was a big item on the bill [cost a lot?].[2] What wonders it worked in me! (25) The most beautiful woman has never been said to display such pretty rosy cheeks that people have noticed in my face.

Listen to what the fourth glass of wine did; it gave me reputation: (30) I was praised for my attractiveness. A young man without a beard has never been given such compliments. The wine made me wise and eloquent. Whatever Frauenlob and [Wolfram von] Eschenbach (35) and Master Gottfried [von Straßburg] spoke was nothing compared to my art and could not be likened to what I said.[3]

The fifth glass of wine was powerful and worked wonders in me. (40) It taught me, without lying, all secrets fully, as if I were a sworn councilman. I began to talk openly about what the emperor, the pope, and the King Soldan [Sultan] (45) were doing. The sixth glass of wine caused more amazing things to happen in me. It seemed to me that I just had arrived from across the sea, from

---

[1] Literally: "misdeed."

[2] Literally: "The bill noticed it clearly.'"

[3] Unusual and highly interesting reference to some of the most famous Middle High German poets. This is the only time in all of Kaufringer's work that he includes a literary historical reference, but it seems rather unlikely that he had a clear idea about his famous thirteenth-century predecessors, so he probably cited them only in an ironic fashion. For a discussion of the idealization of medieval poets as the twelve masters, including Wolfram, Gottfried, and Frauenlob during the late Middle Ages, see Horst Brunner, *Die alten Meister*, 1975.

the lands of the Moors, from Lake Galilee. (50) I knew Jerusalem well. My oh my, what strange tricks described that I had learned. Thank God, how many foreign tricks did I conceive that I had learned among the Greeks. In what fantastic manner did the Emperor, together with his knighthood, honor me when I departed from him. (55)

The seventh glass of wine advised me to fall down on the ground. I said: "Is this the hall of the heroes? Well then, is there anyone who wants to enter a wrestling match with me, or wants to run and jump?" (60) And if there were some who wanted to claim their own stake and intended to fight with me using sharp swords, I would fight them all. In those times you would have seen neither Samson nor Asiel (65; he is mentioned in a genealogy of Simeon as the father of Seraiah, 1 Chronicles 4:35) so strong and so fast as you could observe me then. I jumped from one wall to the other, just like a headless rooster.

Then my innkeeper, an honorable man, (70) said: "Lord, let your rage rest now! Who might be your equal? The strength of all heroes is nothing compared to yours, as one can observe with you. Now, hand me the noble juice, (75) I mean the good wine, and let the guests drink further!"

Truly, you ought to know—he pushed me down on the bench and offered me wine again, and so I drank. (80)

Upon the eighth glass of wine, which I enjoyed there, I told the innkeeper: "Tell me, Sir Innkeeper, whom do you call guest? You seem to me to be as bark compared to silk. (85) You should honorably address me as 'lord' and not as 'guest.' I am the silk, you are the bark. That seems to me to be the real truth. When you call me that (you are my servant), (90) my relatives in England would know of it; then my nephew, the King of France, would also hear about it. And both kings would avenge this fully."

The ninth glass of wine created even more miracles. (95) Although I did not ask for it, I drank so much that tears ran from my eyes, as if I were a child and not a man, so I cried for something that was not my fault. By God's grace, (100) I believed that my dear brother was dead. People had to figure out my remorseful laments and my misery from half uttered words that they could recognize.

The tenth glass of wine had the greatest strength. (105) Just as divine mastership can punish arrogance, so I lost power over my hands and feet because of the effect of the wine. My yapping tongue was tamed, (110) so I sat there like a mute, since the tongue limped ever more in the course of time, so no one could understand me. Hence I had to stop lulling.

The eleventh glass of wine robbed me of the rest of my strength. (115) There was no more melody or song, both had come to a rest [had returned to their previous stage]. The lofty jumps that I had done before I avoided then [no one was seeing me doing them]. The other customers also had to suffer (120) because I was the innkeeper's guest. When all my strength had left me, I would not have been able to defend myself if an ant had pushed me down with its foot. (125) That was the punishment of that [last] drink.

The twelfth glass of wine, called St. John's blessing, gave me wondrous help because the innkeeper and his servants carried me to my usual bedstead (130). They let me rest until the next morning.

Thus I praise the strength of wine over the mastership of words. Roots and stones (135) weigh little against it. Anyone who wants to prove me wrong should argue against me and demonstrate the opposite with his words. I would then help him praise it, (140) if the majority of listeners followed him. These are The Teichner's [Kaufringer's] words.

BIBLIOGRAPHY

Alterskulturen des Mittelalters und der frühen Neuzeit. Akten des 16. Internationalen Kongresses Krems 16. bis 18. Oktober 2006, ed. Elisabeth Vavra. Veröffentlichungen des Instituts für Realienkunde des Mittelalters und der Frühen Neuzeit, 21 (Vienna: Verlag der Österreichischen Akademie der Wissenschaften, 2008).

Autorentypen, ed. Walter Haug and Burghart Wachinger. Fortuna vitrea, 6 (Tübingen: Max Niemeyer, 1991).

Beine, Birgit, *Der Wolf in der Kutte: Geistliche in den Mären des deutschen Mittelalters*. Braunschweiger Beiträge zur deutschen Sprache und Literatur, 2 (Bielefeld: Verlag für Regionalgeschichte, 1999).

Browning, Oscar, *Guelphs & Ghibelline: Short History of Medieval Italy from 1250–1409* (1894; [Charleston, SC]: Nabu Press, 2011).

Brunner, Horst, *Die alten Meister: Studien zu Überlieferung und Rezeption der mittelhochdeutschen Sangspruchdichter im Spätmittelalter und in der frühen Neuzeit*. Münchener Texte und Untersuchungen zur deutschen Literatur des Mittelalters, 54 (Munich: C. H. Beck, 1975).

Classen, Albrecht, "Vom Mære zum Prosa-Schwank des 16. und 17. Jahrhunderts: Tradition und Transformation einer literarischen Gattung vom frühen Mittelalter bis zur Frühneuzeit," *Kontinuitäten und Neuerungen in Textsorten- und Textallianztraditionen vom 13. bis zum 18. Jahrhundert*, ed. Jörg Meier and Peter Ernst. Germanistische Arbeiten zur Sprachgeschichte, 10 (Berlin: Weidler, 2014), 295–321.

———, "Was There a German 'Geoffrey Chaucer' in the Late Middle Ages? The Rediscovery of Heinrich Kaufringer's Verse Narratives as Literary Masterpieces," *Studia Neophilologica* 85.1 (2013): 57–72.

———, review of Gerrit Deutschländer, *Dienen lernen*, 2012, *Sixteenth-Century Journal* XLIV.1 (2013): 307–8.

———, "Männlichkeit und Geschlechts-Identität in der Schwankliteratur des 16. Jahrhunderts," *»Ich bin ein Mann! Wer ist es mehr?« Männlichkeitskonzepte in der deutschen Literatur vom Mittelalter bis zur Gegenwart*, ed. Barbara Hindinger and Martin-M. Langner (Munich: Iudicium, 2011), 66–91.

———, "Laughing in Late-Medieval Verse (*mæren*) and Prose (*Schwänke*) Narratives: Epistemological Strategies and Hermeneutic Explorations," *Laughter in the Middle Ages and Early Modern Times: Epistemology of a Fundamental*

Human Behavior, Its Meaning, and Consequences, ed. id. Fundamentals of Medieval and Early Modern Culture, 5 (Berlin and New York: Walter de Gruyter, 2010), 547–85.

——— (together with Lukas Richter), *Lied und Liederbuch in der Frühen Neuzeit.* Volksliedstudien, 10 (Münster, New York et al.: Waxmann, 2010).

———, *Deutsche Schwankliteratur des 16. Jahrhunderts: Studien zu Martin Montanus, Hans Wilhelm Kirchhof und Michael Lindener.* Koblenz-Landauer Studien zu Geistes-, Kultur- und Bildungswissenschaften, 4 (Trier: Wissenschaftlicher Verlag Trier, 2009).

———, "Love, Marriage, and Sexual Transgressions in Heinrich Kaufringer's Verse Narratives (ca. 1400)," *Discourse on Love, Marriage, and Transgression in Medieval and Early Modern Literature*, ed. Albrecht Classen. Medieval and Renaissance Texts and Studies, 278 (Tempe: Arizona Center for Medieval and Renaissance Studies, 2004 [appeared in 2005]), 289–312.

———, *Verzweiflung und Hoffnung. Die Suche nach der kommunikativen Gemeinschaft in der deutschen Literatur des Mittelalters.* Beihefte zur Mediaevistik, 1 (Frankfurt a.M. et al.: Peter Lang, 2002).

———, *Deutsche Liederbücher des 15. und 16. Jahrhunderts.* Volksliedstudien, 1 (Münster, New York, et al.: Waxmann, 2001).

———, "Mord, Totschlag, Vergewaltigung, Unterdrückung und Sexualität. Liebe und Gewalt in der Welt von Heinrich Kaufringer," *Daphnis* 29.1–2 (2000): 3–36.

———, *The German Volksbuch: A Critical History of a Late-Medieval Genre.* Studies in German Language and Literature, 15 (Lewiston, Queenston, und Lampeter: Edwin Mellen Press, 1995).

Clements, Robert J. and Joseph Gibaldi, *Anatomy of the Novella: The European Tale Collection from Boccaccio and Chaucer to Cervantes* (New York: New York University Press, 1977).

Deutschländer, Gerrit, *Dienen lernen, um zu herrschen: Höfische Erziehung im ausgehenden Mittelalter (1450–1550).* Hallische Beiträge zur Geschichte des Mittelalters und der Frühen Neuzeit, 6 (Berlin: Akademie Verlag, 2012).

Discourses on Love, Marriage, and Transgression in Medieval and Early Modern Literature, ed. Albrecht Classen. Medieval and Renaissance Texts and Studies, 278 (Tempe: Arizona Center for Medieval and Renaissance Studies, 2004).

Ehrismann, Otfrid, with Albrecht Classen, Winder McConnell, et al., *Ehre und Mut, Aventiure und Minne: Höfische Wortgeschichten aus dem Mittelalter* (Munich: Beck, 1995).

Erotic Tales of Medieval Germany, selected and trans. by Albrecht Classen. Second rev. ed. exp. Medieval and Renaissance Texts and Studies, 328 (Tempe: Arizona Center for Medieval and Renaissance Studies, 2007/2009).

Erzählungen des späten Mittelalters und ihr Weiterleben in Literatur und Volksdichtung bis zur Gegenwart: Sagen, Märchen, Exempel und Schwänke, with a commentary ed. by Lutz Röhrich. 2 vols. (Berlin and Munich: Franke, 1962 and 1967).

Fischer, Hanns, *Studien zur deutschen Märendichtung*. Second rev. exp. ed., prepared by Johannes Janota (Tübingen: Max Niemeyer, 1983).

Fischer, Hubertus, *Ritter, Schiff und Dame: Mauritius von Craûn: Text und Kontext*. Beiträge zur älteren Literaturgeschichte (Heidelberg: Universitätsverlag Winter, 2006).

Friedrich, Udo, "Metaphorik des Spiels und Reflexion des Erzählens bei Heinrich Kaufringer," *Internationales Archiv für Sozialgeschichte der deutschen Literatur* 21.1 (1996): 1–30.

Grubmüller, Kurt, *Die Ordnung, der Witz und das Chaos: Eine Geschichte der europäischen Novellistik im Mittelalter: Fabliaux - Märe - Novelle* (Tübingen: Niemeyer, 2006).

Haase, H.-W., "Die Theodicee-Legende vom Engel und dem Eremiten," Ph.D. dissertation. Georg-August Universität Göttingen 1966.

Hartmann von Aue, *Erec*. Mit einem Abdruck der neuen Wolfenbütteler und Zwettler Erec-Fragmente, ed. Albert Leitzmann, continued by Ludwig Wolff. 7th ed. by Kurt Gärtner. Altdeutsche Textbibliothek, 39 (Tübingen: Niemeyer, 2006).

Heinzle, Joachim, "Kleine Anleitung zum Gebrauch des Märenbergriffs," *Kleinere Erzählformen im Mittelalter: Paderborner Colloquium 1987*, ed. Klaus Grubmüller, L. Peter Johnson, and Hans-Hugo Steinhoff. Schriften der Universitäts-Gesamthochschule-Paderborn. Reihe Sprach- und Literaturwissenschaft, 10 (Paderborn, Munich, et al.: Ferdinand Schöningh, 1988), 45–48.

Jean d'Arras, *Melusine; or, the Noble History of Lusignan*, trans. and with an intro. by Donald Maddox and Sara Sturm-Maddox (University Park, PA: The Pennsylvania State University Press, 2012).

Kaufringer, Heinrich, *Werke*, ed. Paul Sappler. Vol. I: *Text*. Vol. II: *Indices* (Tübingen: Max Niemeyer, 1972).

Kavanagh, Thomas M., *Dice, Cards, Wheels: A Different History of French Culture* (Philadelphia: University of Pennsylvania Press, 2005).

Konrad von Würzburg, *Partonopier und Meliur* ed. Karl Bartsch, rpt. Deutsche Neudrucke. Reihe: Texte des Mittelalters (1871; Berlin: Walter de Gruyter, 1970).

Making of the Couple: The Social Function of Short-Form Medieval Narrative. A Symposium, ed. Flemming G. Andersen and Morten Nøjgaard (Odense: Odense University Press, 1991).

Mauritius von Craûn, ed. Heimo Reinitzer. Altdeutsche Textbibliothek, 113 (Tübingen: Max Niemeyer, 2000).

Mihm, Arend., *Überlieferung und Verbreitung der Märendichtung im Spätmittelalter* (Heidelberg: Carl Winter Universitätsverlag, 1967).

Milliman, Paul, "Games and Pasttimes," *Handbook of Medieval Culture*, ed. Albrecht Classen (Berlin and Boston: Walter de Gruyter, forthcoming).

Niewöhner, Heinrich, "Pseudoteichnerisches in der Handschrift Berlin Ms. Germ. Fol. 564," *Beiträge zur Geschichte der deutschen Sprache und Literatur* (Halle) 75 (1953): 391–414.

Novellistik im Mittelalter: Märendichtung, ed., trans., and commentary by Klaus Grubmüller. Bibliothek des Mittelalters, 23 (Frankfurt a. M.: Deutscher Klassiker Verlag, 1996).

Nusser, Peter, *Deutsche Literatur: Eine Sozial- und Kulturgeschichte. Vom Mittelalter bis zur Frühen Neuzeit* [vol. 1] (Darmstadt: Wissenschaftliche Buchgesellschaft, 2012).

Obermaier, Sabine, *Das Fabelbuch als Rahmenerzählung: Intertextualität und Intratextualität als Wege zur Interpretation des Buchs der Beispiele der alten Weisen Antons von Pforr*. Beihefte zum Euphorion, 48 (Heidelberg: Universitätsverlag Winter, 2004).

Old Age in the Middle Ages and the Renaissance: Interdisciplinary Approaches to a Neglected Topic, ed. Albrecht Classen. Fundamentals of Medieval and Early Modern Culture, 2 (Berlin and New York: Walter de Gruyter, 2007).

Resler, Michael, "Der Stricker," *German Writers and Works of the High Middle Ages: 1170–1280*, ed. James Hardin and Will Hasty. Dictionary of Literary Biography, 138 (Detroit, Washington, DC, and London: Gale Research, 1994), 117–32.

Ruh, Kurt, "Kaufringers Erzählung von der 'Unschuldigen Mörderin'," *Interpretation und Edition deutscher Texte des Mittelalters: Festschrift für John Asher zum 60. Geburtstag*, ed. Kathryn Smits, Werner Besch, and Victor Lange (Berlin: Erich Schmidt, 1981), 164–77.

Rushing, James A., "Erec's Uxuriousness," *Discourses on Love, Marriage, and Transgression in Medieval and Early Modern Literature*, ed. Albrecht Classen. Medieval and Renaissance Texts and Studies, 278 (Tempe: Arizona Center for Medieval and Renaissance Studies, 2004, appeared in 2005), 163–80.

Sappler, Paul, "Kaufringer, Heinrich," *Die deutsche Literatur des Mittelalters: Verfasserlexikon*, ed. Kurt Ruh et al. Second completely rev. ed. (Berlin and New York: Walter de Gruyter, 1982), cols. 1076–85.

Schirmer, Karl-Heinz, *Stil- und Motivuntersuchungen zur mittelhochdeutschen Versnovelle*. Hermaea, Germanistische Forschungen, Neue Folge, 26 (Tübingen: Niemeyer, 1969).

Schneider, Karin, *Die deutschen Handschriften der Bayerischen Staatsbibliothek München: Die mittelalterlichen Handschriften aus Cgm 888–4000*. Second ed. (Wiesbaden: Harrassowitz, 1991).

———, *Die deutschen Handschriften der Bayerischen Staatsbibliothek München: Cgm 201–350*. Second ed. (Wiesbaden: Harrassowitz, 1970).

Schwarzbaum, H., "Engel und Eremit," *Enzyklopädie des Märchens: Handwörterbuch zur historischen und vergleichenden Erzählforschung*, ed. Kurt Ranke et al. Vol. 3 (Berlin and New York: Walter de Gruyter, 1981), 1438–46.

Simmons, Cynthia Lynn, "Tales by Heinrich Kaufringer: A Discussion and Translation of Selected Works," M.A. thesis, The University of Texas at Austin, 1985.

Stede, Marga, *Schreiben in der Krise: Die Texte des Heinrich Kaufringer*. Literatur – Imagination – Realität, 5 (Trier: Wissenschaftlicher Verlag Trier, 1993).

Steinmetz, Ralf-Henning, "Heinrich Kaufringers selbstbewusste Laienmoral," *Beiträge zur Geschichte der deutschen Sprache und Literatur* 121.1 (1999): 47–74.

Strasser, Ingrid, *Vornovellistisches Erzählen: Mittelhochdeutsche Mären bis zur Mitte des 14. Jahrhunderts und altfranzösische Fabliaux* (Vienna: Fassbaender, 1989).

Till Eulenspiegel: His Adventures, trans., with intro. and notes, by Paul Oppenheimer (New York and London: Routledge, 2001).

Tolan, John, *Petrus Alfonsi and His Medieval Readers* (Gainesville, Tallahassee, et al.: University Press of Florida, 1993).

Vogt, Ulrich, *Der Würfel ist gefallen: 5000 Jahre rund um den Kubus* (Hildesheim and New York: Olms, 2012).

The Vulgate Bible. Vol. III: *The Poetical Books. Douay-Rheims Translation*, ed. Edgar Swift with Angela M. Kinney. Dumbarton Oaks Medieval Library (Cambridge, MA, and London: Harvard University Press, 2011).

Willers, Michaela, *Heinrich Kaufringer als Märenautor: Das Oeuvre des cgm 270* (Berlin: Logos Verlag, 2002).

Wittenwiler, Heinrich, *Der Ring: Text – Übersetzung – Kommentar*. Nach der Münchener Handschrift herausgegeben, übersetzt und erläutert von Werner Röcke unter Mitarbeit von Annika Goldenbaum (Berlin and Boston: Walter de Gruyter, 2012).

Wolf, Jürgen, "Konrad Bollstatter und die Augsburger Geschichtsschreibung: Die letzte Schaffensperiode," *Zeitschrift für deutsches Altertum und deutsche Literatur* 125 (1996): 51–86.

Words of Love and Love of Words in the Middle Ages and the Renaissance, ed. Albrecht Classen. Medieval and Renaissance Texts and Studies, 347 (Tempe: Arizona Center for Medieval and Renaissance Studies, 2008).

Ziegeler, Hans-Joachim, "Maere," *Reallexikon der deutschen Literaturwissenschaft*, ed. Harald Fricke. Vol. II: *H–O* (Berlin and New York: Walter de Gruyter, 2000), 517–20.

———, *Erzählen im Spätmittelalter: Mären im Kontext von Minnereden, Bispeln und Romanen*. Münchener Texte und Untersuchungen zur deutschen Literatur des Mittelalters, 87 (Munich: Artemis, 1985).

INDEX

Adelheid, xii
Alfonsi, Petrus, viii
Angerer, Hans, xii
Anton von Pforr, ix
Asiel, 146
Augustine, St., 105–06
Beheim, Michel, x
Berthold von Regensburg, xiv, xviii–xix
Boccaccio, Giovanni, vii, x, xvi, xxii, xxiv–xxv
Bollstatter, Konrad, xiv
Bote, Hermen, 70
Bracciolini, Poggio, vii
Buch der Beispiele der alten Weisen, ix
Cent Nouvelles Nouvelles, xxii
Chaucer, Geoffrey, vii, ix–x, xvi, xxii–xxiv
children, 95–98, 113–14
Counselors (see also lawyers), 121–22, 143
David, King, 54
Directorium vitae humanae, ix
Disciplina clericalis, viii
drunkenness, 145–47
exemplum, viii
fable, viii
fabliaux, ix
fashion, 139–41
Folz, Hans, x
Frauenlob, 145
Freidank, xviii
Frey, Wilhelm, ix
Fröschel von Leidnitz, xviii
Gernpaß, Michel (?), xviii
Ghibelines, 117
Gottfried von Strassburg, 145
Groninger, Peter, xvii
Guelphs, 117
Heinrich von Pforzen, xvii
Jews, 7–10, 133–35
John of Capua, ix

Judas, 92
Kalfla wa-Dimna, ix
Kirchhof, Hans Wilhelm, ix
Der König vom Odenwald, xix
Konrad, der arme, xvii
Laber, xvii
lawyers (see also counselors), 109–11, 117
Liederbücher, x
Lindener, Michael, ix
madness, 102–03
Marguerite de Navarre, vii, xxv
Mauritius von Craûn, xxi
mæren, viii
Mönch von Salzburg, x, xviii
Morgenrot, xix
Oswald von Wolkenstein, x
Panchatantra, ix
Pauli, Johannes, ix
Pfaffe Amis, viii
Raminger, Hans, xvii–xviii
rape, 35–36
Rosenplüt, Hans, x
Sacchetti, Franco, vii
Samson, 54, 146
Schmieher, Peter, xvii, xix
Schuhmann, Valentin, ix
Schwank/Schwänke, viii, ix, xv
Seven Deadly Sins, 123–26
Simeon, 146
Solomon, 54
The Stricker, vii
Suchenwirt, Peter, xvii–xviii
Teichner, xiv–xv, xix–xx, xxv
Till Eulenspiegel/Till Eulenspiegel, viii, 70
Werder, Jörg, xiv
Wickram, Georg (Jörg), ix
Wilhalm von Orlens, xiv, xix
wine, 145–47
Wolfram von Eschenbach, 145